Get It Sold!

A proven method
for selling your home
FOR TOP DOLLAR

2ND EDITION
BY SEBASTIAN "SEB" FREY, REALTOR®
CALIFORNIA REAL ESTATE BROKER
LIC. 01369847

SEBFREY.COM

Copyright © 2021 by Sebastian Frey
All rights reserved. No part of this book may be reproduced, scanned,
or distributed in any printed or electronic form without permission.
First Edition: January 2017
Second Edition: January 2021
Written and Edited in the United States of America
ISBN: 978-1-63752-602-6

To My Wife Rocio
and My Two Boys
Aiden and Evan.
You Mean the World to Me.

Table of Contents

PREFACE

1 THE BEAUTY & CHALLENGE OF REAL ESTATE — 1

2 METHODS OF SELLING A HOME — 3

3 IT'S A NUMBERS GAME — 9
- The Four Major Success Factors — 10

4 PLANNING TO SELL — 11
- Selling and Buying — 13
- Emotional Challenges — 16

5 MARKETING YOUR HOME — 20

6 THE PRICE IS RIGHT — 34
- The CMA (Comparative Market Analysis) — 40
- Pricing Unique and Luxury Properties — 54

7 PREPARING YOUR HOME FOR THE MARKET — 60
- Concierge Services — 65
- The Fabulous Four - Preparation Tasks — 66
- Pre-Sale Inspections — 71
- Creative Ways to Finance Home Preparation — 73

8 STAGING — 81
- Staging by the Numbers — 82

9 YOUR REPRESENTATION — 86
- Questions to Ask Prospective Agents — 87
- Communicating with your Agent — 90
- Being Your Own Agent (Selling FSBO) — 91
- Discount Brokers — 94
- Dual Agency ("Double-Ending" the deal) — 96

A Few Words about Commissions — 99

10 ON THE MARKET — 103

The Perfect Home Sale Schedule — 105
Handling Showings — 109
Tenant Occupied Homes — 112
Top Tips on Showing the Home — 114
Selling your Home in a Tough Market — 115

11 ALL ABOUT OFFERS — 118

Negotiation is An Art Form — 132

12 THE HOME STRETCH — 134

13 THE LAST WORD(S) — 142

Preface

I've written this book for California homeowners who are contemplating the sale of their home. A lot of what you'll find herein doubtless applies to home sales in all 50 states, but I'm a California real estate broker; all my real estate sales experience lies within the borders of the Golden state. Homeowners everywhere will benefit from reading this book, but it is especially pertinent for those thinking of selling a home in California.

If you're thinking about selling your home – and I'm guessing you are, since you're reading this book on how to get your home *sold* – you're probably going through a whole range of emotions. Selling a home is usually a significant milestone in life, and it's one that most people reach only a very few times (if ever).

In fact, selling a home often goes hand in hand with a major change in life: marriage, divorce, death, a new child coming, children leaving for college, job loss, or moving to a new job opportunity across town or across the country. Because selling a home is so often tied to one or more major life events, the stresses often overlap and can become, at times, overwhelming.

Sometimes, though, selling a home is purely a financial decision, such as an investment property you've decided to sell to free up capital for some other use. Regardless: for most people, selling a home certainly isn't an every-day occurrence, and unfamiliarity with the process can lead to a lot of headaches and anxiety.

If you're feeling unsure about how best to proceed with the sale of your home, you're in the right place. In this book, I've worked to include the most important things you need to understand about selling your home quickly, but for top dollar – with the least amount of hassle, risk, and uncertainty.

But why write another book about it? Aren't there hundreds of other books available on the subject?

Of course there are – maybe thousands, even! But many of these books are outdated, dull as toast, not specific to California, and are of limited use in the 21st century real estate market. The world is changing quickly, and the way real estate is bought and *sold* is changing even faster. I am herein offering a series of fresh ideas and an aggressive strategy and tactics for maximizing your net dollar upon sale in today's hyper-connected market.

For many people, the idea of selling their home fills them with dread. There's so much uncertainty: how long will the home take to sell? Will it sell at all? What can I do to net top dollar and maximize my cash-out at closing? Just how much money will I walk away with? This book is designed to allay your concerns and show you how selling your home can be easy – even fun!

Not only can it be fun, selling your home can be predictable: you can know how much your home should sell for, how much you'll walk away with at closing, and even how long it will take for the property to close - before you ever put your home on the market.

I truly believe homeowners such as yourself should be rewarded for the time, money, effort, and love they've invested into their homes. You deserve every dollar of value you can get out of your house when you go to sell it - and still make your home's buyer feel like they're getting a great deal. That's my goal for every home sale I'm a part of.

Have you ever wondered how and why some people are so happy and excited to be selling their home, while others are on the verge of despair? A lot of it has to do with the difference in *how* the home is **sold**. If you follow the advice in this book, you'll understand what needs to happen so that you're in the former group of sellers, rather than the latter.

As you go through this book, you may have questions which the book doesn't answer. If that's the case, I invite you to log on to my website which contains tons of resources and information for home sellers: SebFrey.com. You'll find a wealth of more detailed information there about the home sale process. And of course, you're always welcome to contact me directly to answer any real estate related questions you may have; my contact info is all over the web site.

Now, without further ado, let's get started!

1
The Beauty & Challenge of Real Estate

Homeownership is a two-sided coin: it provides an amazing vehicle for wealth preservation and creation, but at the same time, has significant drawbacks as an investment. But a home is more than just an investment: it's an essential. Shelter is one of the very most basic human needs, and as such will always have intrinsic value, in any market, at any time.

As an investment, real estate does have a number of drawbacks, such as ongoing maintenance, property taxes, insurance costs, tenant hassles, and the like. When it comes to selling your investment, it also has a significant challenge: it is not a liquid asset. You cannot turn it into cash with the click of a button on a computer screen. Selling real estate can take considerable time, and typically has a much higher transaction cost than say selling off some stocks.

Typically, a home provides both shelter and investment benefits. Many "investment" homes were once occupied by the owners, and they'll feel some emotional attachment to them. Regardless of whether you live in the home presently or not, you may have lived there for a long time and have made a lot of cherished memories in it.

The home you're thinking of selling likely means a lot to you. It means a lot more than a mere collection of boards and nails, shingles, plumbing, and wires heaped on a plot of dirt. Not only that, it's also (probably) your single biggest financial asset. What you do with your house - and how much you sell it for - is very important to you, in more ways than one.

You've chosen to invest quite a lot into your home – not just money, but time and sweat too. It's completely different from the stock market, where there's not a lot you can do to enhance the price of your shares. The price goes up or down, no matter what you do, and all you can do is buy and sell at the right (or wrong) time.

Real estate, however, is quite a different animal. Your home is an investment where <u>what you do with it can dramatically affect its market price</u>. This is a double-edged sword: improperly developed and cared for, your property can become devalued. However, with proper attention, good upkeep, and an eye toward the future, a smart homeowner can increase his home's value. You can do this over the time you own the property, or *just prior to putting it on the market*. Either way, the ability to significantly enhance a home's value is one of the things that can make real estate such an amazing investment for a family.

This book will provide you with all the essential information I feel you need to know to knock it out of the park with the sale of your home. After years in the business, I've developed a clear and straightforward method of selling homes. This book takes you through the steps of my method and helps you to understand why I strongly recommend homes be sold using these techniques.

2
Methods of Selling a Home

When most people think of selling their home, they think of a Realtor® pounding a "For Sale" sign into their yard, doing open houses, and private showings conducted over a period of weeks or months before being able to find a buyer. This is the way that most homes  have traditionally been sold in the United States, and in fact, it's the most common way homes are sold today.

But it's certainly not the *only* way to sell a home. There are in fact a number of different ways to sell your home, and I will touch on them here in this chapter.

SELL TO AN INVESTOR

Have you seen those "We buy houses" signs around town? Nowadays you're more likely to see them on Facebook or in a Google search result, but it's the same kind of buyer. These "investors" are typically looking for homes they can buy below market value, fix up, and sell for a profit – usually a pretty handsome profit.

These investors cannot pay you top dollar for your home – their business model precludes it, because they have to make a profit that an owner-buyer will not be looking for. However, they do offer an easy sale, with a closing date on your timeline. They'll usually let you turn over the house with whatever treasure (junk) you want to leave behind. They also won't expect you to do any repairs either.

Selling to an investor is usually as simple as signing a contract, then handing over the keys on closing day and picking up a check. Yes, you may end up leaving tens of thousands — or even a hundred thousand — dollars or more on the table, but if certainty, ease, and convenience are the most important things to you, then selling to an investor is something you can consider.

I work with a lot of cash buyer investors! If you are thinking of going this route, please reach out to me. You'll find my contact info plastered all over my website at SebFrey.com

SELL TO AN IBUYER

A few years back, a "new" way of selling homes popped up: the iBuyer. I presume that the "i" stands for Internet, because these are mostly online companies that specialize in getting you "instant offers" on your home. These firms are usually backed by big hedge funds and institutional investors, and purport to use advanced software which enables them to make very competitive offers.

When these firms first came onto the scene, they were often limited to specific geographies (e.g. Phoenix, Arizona) and would only buy certain types of homes (homes no more than 40 years old, with a maximum purchase price of $500,000, etc.).

Today, iBuyers are making offers on a much wider array of homes. Not every iBuyer operates in every market, and not every iBuyer will purchase every kind of home. Their marketing promises they are able to make an offer that nets a seller very close to the same amount they would end up getting if they sold the "traditional" way homes are sold in the U.S. – minus all the hassle and uncertainty.

Because there's big money behind these iBuyers, part of the strategy is to funnel business (and profits) into ancillary enterprises, such as mortgage, title/escrow, insurance, and home improvement. They create a vertical stack of businesses to extract profit at various points in the sale and resale of a property. The claim is that by doing so, they don't need as big a margin as the old school "mom and pop" investor.

Despite all the initial hype, iBueyrs still represent a very small part of the market, years after coming onto the scene. In fact, less than 1% of all homes are sold to iBuyers, acording to the NAR 2020 Profile of Home Buyers and Sellers. If you're curious about getting an offer from an iBuyer, the most well-known iBuyers operating today are OfferPad, Zillow Offers, Knock, Keller Offers, OpenDoor, Orchard, and RedfinNow.

AUCTIONS

You may be surprised to learn that in some countries, most homes are sold at auction. However, in the United States, relatively few homes are this way. In fact, selling a home at auction has soemthing of a stigma attached to it, as most of the homes sold at auction have, historically, been "distressed" properties (foreclosures and the like).

However, there are a number of auction houses that sell real estate in the United States, and not all of them deal in distressed property. In fact, there are some luxury auction firms as well.

Selling via auciton has some attractive aspects to it. One is that you'll have a "date certain" that the home will be sold. Another is that with an auction, all sales are final – at least, buyers are typically not allowed to get their deposit back, should they fail to close the sale for whatever reason. With an auction format, you will have multiple parties bidding on your property, so there is at least some competition among buyers for your home, which should drive the price up.

If you're considering selling by auction, you can look into the various real estate auction companies operating in the United States. These include Auction.com, Hubzu.com, Williams and Willians, Platinum Luxury Auctions, and Elite Auctions are a few you can check into.

SELL ON YOUR OWN

There's a whole section of this book dedicated to the ins-and-outs of selling a home on your own. I don't want to spoil that whole section for you, but I'll point out that 8% of all homes sold in 2020 were sold "by owner" – but this is down from 15% of all homes sold by owner in the early 1980s.

While selling "by owner" is not an especially popular method of selling a home (particularly in California, for whatever reason), it is certainly a viable prospect and something you could consider, especially if you already know somebody who wants to, and is capable of, buying yor home.

SELL WITH A REAL ESTATE BROKER

About 89% of homes sold in the United States are sold with the help of a real estate agent or broker, according to the NAR 2020

Profile of Home Buyers and Sellers. However, not every agent and broker sells homes the same way, or for the same cost to the seller and buyer.

There are flat-fee brokers, discount brokers, limited service brokers, and, of course, traditional full-service real estate brokers like myself. Not only am I broker, I am also a Realtor®. The National Association of Realtors (NAR) is the largest trade association in the United States, with over 1.2 million members at the time of this writing.

Selling your home using the services of a real estate professional is the most popular way to get a home sold. Despite the cost of the commission, it appears that homeowners have found this to be the best way, on balance, to get their homes *sold*.

Contrary to what you may have heard, all real estate agents are not the same. Most have only been in business for a few years and have sold only a handful of homes.

Much of the rest of this book contains years of wisdom about home selling that I've absorbed – and I've absorbed it the hard way, in the trenches, helping all kinds of families buy and sell a bewildering array of home types, in markets that were stone cold, blistering hot, and every degree in between.

In the following pages, I'll share my method for selling homes, in somewhat exhaustive detail. I'll dive deep enough into it so that you understand what's important about every aspect of the method I've developed. Now, let's begin our exploration of my method, and how to *Get It Sold!*

The Goal of My Method

The goal of my method is quite simple: to sell a home quickly, easily, and for the very highest price possible, while reducing uncertainty, hassle, and risk. While the process, the mechanics, of selling a home can be complicated, in the end, it comes down to the basics. The purpose of this book is to show you how to: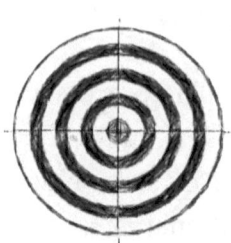

1) Enhance your home's value as perceived by the buying public. The greater *value* people see in your home, the higher the *price* they'll pay for it.

2) Shorten the time it takes to sell your home. As they say in sales, "time kills deals" - the shorter the process is, the more likely it is you'll have a happy, favorable result. A rapid sale is important for a number of reasons, but one of the big ones is that **homes which sell faster sell for more money** compared to those which take weeks or months to sell.

3) Close the sale without drama, on schedule.

4) Complete the sale with the greatest amount of cash flowing to you, including the cost of sale and the work you put into the home getting it ready for sale.

In most cases, folks sell their homes because they need the money locked up inside it for something more important to them. If that's the case, you owe it to yourself to wring every dollar you can out of your home upon the sale. Helping you achieve that is what this book is all about.

3
It's a Numbers Game

There is one thing that I advise all sellers to keep in mind, and it's that selling your home is a numbers game. There are a lot of numbers involved in selling your home. The first number everyone wants to know is: how much can I sell my house for? The answer to that question is, honestly: it depends on a lot of other factors. The truth is, <u>the way that you prepare, price, market, and negotiate the sale of a home will have a great impact on the final sale price of any home.</u>

You know the saying: every little bit helps. That's also very true when it comes to getting a home **sold** at premium pricing. To get the best price for your property, you want to stack the odds - bit by bit - so that they're completely in your favor, leaving as little to chance as possible.

Throughout this book, I'll point out where taking care of a few simple - and often free or very inexpensive - things can potentially have a huge impact on the final net to the seller upon sale. I'll also go over dozens of other tweaks which, when added up, will further boost the numbers in your favor: social media sharing, web traffic, media exposure, open house attendance, buyer inquiries, private showings, offers, and ultimately, the highest price with the best terms possible on the sale of your home.

My method is designed entirely around the proposition of doing everything that can be done to maximize the sale price (and net proceeds to the seller). This is achieved by being deliberate and systematic in the approach, by taking all the small steps that lead up to a big number for the seller at the closing table.

The Four Major Success Factors

After selling hundreds of homes over 18+ years in business, I've concluded that the four most important factors to successfully selling a home quickly and for the very biggest number are:

1. Marketing (and *pre-marketing*)
2. Price
3. Condition
4. Negotiation

I work with my clients to ensure that we have these key elements going for us to get the home ***sold*** in the least amount of time for the highest price. We'll take a detailed look at each of these elements in the next few chapters.

4
Planning to Sell

The most well-executed sales happen with considerable planning, with many decisions large and small made along the way. The biggest decision, however, comes *before* you begin the work of getting your home **sold**. Before anything else, you need to make the decision to sell – and for most people, that's not a decision that comes easily nor is made lightly.

I talk to a lot of people about selling their home, and one thing that's very common is *uncertainty*. Putting a home up for sale is a big decision, and I find that most homeowners who think about moving do so for *years* before they finally set the ball rolling.

I can't tell you how many times I've had people tell me "I'll be moving next year" – and then next year comes around, and now they say they'll be moving in 3-4 years. If you're having a difficult time deciding to keep or sell your home, you're in one crowded boat!

Some people hesitate to move because they aren't sure they are selling at the best time. Obviously, it's best to sell at the peak of the market, right? That's true, but the reality is that you can never know for sure ahead of time when you're at the top of the market.

As I mentioned earlier, in most cases, the decision to sell is ultimately triggered by a change in life circumstances (death, divorce, marriage, children, job, etc.). And you should also know, sales volume is fairly consistent, in good markets and bad. No matter the market, rest assured *there is a buyer for your home.*

I remember the mortgage crisis of 2008 very well. This was arguably the worst real estate market for sellers since the Great Depression. But even then, a well-priced and well-presented home could garner multiple offers in a short time and sell well over list price.

Moving Factoids

TOP FIVE REASONS PEOPLE MOVE:
1. Get a new or better home/apartment (15%)
2. A family reason (besides marriage or starting a new household 15%)
3. Another housing reason (other than wanting a new or cheaper house, better neighborhood, etc.14%)
4. To establish their own new household (10%)
5. New job or job transfer (10%)

BETWEEN 2013 AND 2014:
- About 1 in 9 people changed homes
- The suburbs had a net gain of 2.2 million movers, while principal cities had a net loss of 1.7 million.
- Renters moved a lot! 24.5% of all people living in renter-occupied housing units lived elsewhere one-year prior. **The mover rate of all people living in owner-occupied housing units was 5.0 percent.**
- New job or job transfer was the highest job-related reason for moving at 9.7 percent.

(Source: U.S. Census Bureau)

Selling and Buying

As I just mentioned, the decision to sell a home usually revolves around a life event, but one thing that hopefully doesn't change is that you'll still need a place to live. Many owners are reluctant to sell their home because the question arises: well, where do I go next?

That's a very personal question and one only you can answer. But I can take some of the worry off your shoulders and tell you that people sell their homes and buy another every day.

There are a few ways to handle this, and yes, it can be a bit of a juggle. It's certainly a very manageable process, but it's one that will require a little more planning. Let's explore some of the options here.

MAKING CONTINGENT OFFERS

Historically, most sellers who need to sell-then-buy would first put their home on the market, and then look for a replacement home. They make the sale of their current home contingent on finding (and usually closing) on a replacement home. They also make the purchase of the replacement home contingent on the successful closing of their current home.

This puts you at a disadvantage on two fronts. First, you need to find a buyer who is OK with going into contract on a home where you, the seller, has an "out," because if you can't find a replacement home, you can cancel the contract and the buyer has to start all over again. Next, the seller of whatever home *you* want to buy will have to worry about two closings – successfully closing the sale of your current home, and the new home you want to buy from them.

To get your contingent offer accepted on your replacement property, you may have to pay a "contingency tax." To overcome that seller's concerns around accepting your contingent offer, you may have to offer a higher price. This is especially true if there are other competing offers on the table – which is often the case.

While I do believe in selling for the highest price possible, I also believe in paying the least amount possible when you buy. However, with this "contingency tax," the "least amount possible" is probably more than if you had no such contingency.

And that's important to keep in mind when you're evaluating some of the other options for the "sell-then-buy" scenario. All of them have costs, but at the end of the day, they may actually be the less expensive options out there.

BRIDGE FINANCING

Another option you can explore is bridge financing. With bridge financing, a lender loans you the equity you have in your current home so you can use it as the down payment on your new home – before you sell your existing home. Then, after you close the purchase of the new home, you sell your old home and repay the bridge loan, and the loan to whatever bank holds your mortgage (if you have one).

Of course, bridge financing isn't free, and qualifying for a bridge loan may require a higher income than you have. You may also end up making monthly payments on three loans: your old mortgage, your new mortgage, and the bridge loan.

While there is a cost to bridge financing, it may end up costing you less than the aforementioned "contingency tax" while also allowing you to make a stronger, cleaner offer which is more likely to beat any competition – without the need to greatly exceed competing offer prices.

HOME EQUITY LINE OF CREDIT

Instead of using a bridge loan to tap your home's equity, you could get a HELOC – a Home Equity Line of Credit. You'd need to do this before you put your home on the market, and it will require an appraisal and other origination fees. You should be able to leverage up to 80% of your home's value using a HELOC, subtracting out whatever you presently owe on it.

Let's say your home is worth $1 million, and you owe $500,000 on it. 80% of $1,000,000 is $800,000 – but you owe $500,000 so you could expect to get a HELOC for $300,000 – which you can then use as the down payment on your next home. Some lenders may allow a HELOC up to 90% of value, so in this scenario, you might be able to get as much as $400,000 for a down payment (and closing costs) using this approach.

IBUYERS

I covered iBuyers in Chapter 2 in the discussion of the various methods for getting your home sold. I mention them again because they may provide an attractive option specifically in the sell-then-buy scenario.

There are some iBuyers who have tailored programs specifically for people who want to sell their current home and buy a new one. Though there are new entrants into this space all the time, and surely some of today's iBuyers will be gone tomorrow, two of these companies which purportedly have programs tailored for this are Knock.com and EasyKnock.com.

I personally have yet to work with these companies (or any iBuyer, really). However, as they are for-profit ventures, I expect that they charge a handsome premium for their services – in exchange for convenience, certainty, and much less stress.

Emotional Challenges

If you thought buying a home was an emotional roller coaster, you should try selling one! The experience will be much more emotionally charged if you're selling out of some financial hardship, the dissolution of a marriage, or loss of a loved one.

The process is emotionally draining in many ways and on many levels. Preparing to sell the home where you've lived for years, perhaps where you've raised your children with their successive height marks still on a wall – it's tough. Or if you're selling your parents' home, sorting through a lifetime of their possessions and deciding what to do with them brings up a whole host of feelings that can be hard to deal with.

And that's just for starters. You still have the unenviable task of finding an agent, figuring out what you need to do to get your house ready for sale, the grunt work of preparing it for market, deal with buyers, open houses, negotiating, and managing the transaction through the closing process. And then when all is said and done, you'll usually have to move somewhere new! It's no surprise that most people take a long time to finally pull the trigger and put the home up for sale.

I mention all this because I want you to be aware of the cascade of emotion that most sellers go through. I also want to let you know that it's perfectly normal. If you want my advice: *embrace it*. Make it a family event; home is all about family, after all. Get all the family on board if you can and have them help you shoulder the burden. Making a move like this does have the potential to bring families back together again.

As a seller, you'll find many things to worry about, large and small. Fortunately, many of them exist only in your imagination and won't ever come to pass. When you're working with the right real estate agent, much of the heavy lifting will be taken off your shoulders.

My mission when working with home sellers is always the same: to sell the home for the highest price possible, as quickly as can be, with the least amount of hassle, risk, and uncertainty.

To successfully meet my objective, I need to have the sellers on board with the process – and that means educating them. I've found that a great deal of my client's stress comes from simply not knowing and feeling out of control. By educating them about the process and guiding them to a great outcome, the stress melts away and my clients usually find (to their surprise) that there's fun to be had in selling their home.

The joy comes from the ability to reach a goal – to hit a big milestone in life and knock it out of the park. Taking the bull by the horns and seizing the day, making your new future happen – the feeling of accomplishment is very empowering. The experience can be very fun, rewarding, and even cathartic.

In my discussions with potential sellers, I am often asked if *I* think *they* should sell their home. It seems like a logical question, but isn't that kind of like a hen asking a fox if it's OK to leave the henhouse door unlocked at night?

You might think I'm the wrong person to ask that question – but when I'm asked, you may be surprised to hear that I often advise my clients *not* to sell a home. As we say in real estate, "you make money when you buy, not when you sell" (you just get the cash when you sell). Real estate works best as a long-term investment, and typically, the longer you own it, the greater the benefit to you.

I usually get that question when a seller hasn't made a clear decision to sell – and if a seller isn't clear on their "why," they usually end up sitting tight. I've found that when a client is truly motivated, and clear on their need to sell, they won't ask me if I think they should sell - they already know the answer.

However, a lot of folks who truly want, or need, to sell their home still have a high level of anxiety about making the decision to pull the trigger. To these people, I say this: any decision you make can prove to be good or bad, depending on *how well the decision is executed, and the choices you make* **after** *taking the decision.*

Selling the family home so you can buy a Ferrari and blow the rest on a crazy weekend in Vegas could show that you made a bad choice. Likewise, the decision *not* to sell could prove to be poor, if for example you later lose the home to foreclosure or the price drops precipitously and doesn't recover before you genuinely *need* to sell.

The wisdom of selling or holding on to a home may only become fully apparent years down the road. My best advice is to make your decision *consciously* and then capitalize on it by continuing to make smart choices about your housing needs and investment strategy.

DOUBLE DOWN ON SELLING YOUR HOME

Once you've made the decision to sell your home, my suggestion is to double down on that, mentally, emotionally, physically, and financially. Grit your teeth and put your shoulder to the grindstone. You know what they say: if you're going to do something, *might as well do it right*.

Doing it right means following the guidance you'll receive in this book. Don't blink, don't think twice – *just do it*. It may seem like a lot of work, but with the help and encouragement of a professional real estate broker such as myself, you'll find that it all will go much more quickly and easily than it first appears.

Are you ready to begin? Then let's get moving!

5
Marketing your Home

To quote the American Marketing Association, marketing is "the activity, set of institutions, and processes for creating, communicating, delivering, and exchanging offerings that have value for customers, clients, partners, and society at large."

That's a pretty unexciting quote from an organization that you'd think would be all about crafting catchy buzz lines, wouldn't you say?

As I mentioned in Chapter 3, one of the major factors for a successful top-dollar sale of a home is marketing. The goal of my marketing plan is simple: establish your home as a "must see" property in the minds of as many potential buyers as possible.

I've seen a lot of half-assed marketing for homes out there – you probably have, too. Amateur photography (often blurry and shot with a mobile phone), brief and bland description of the home – and many times, *no description of the home whatsoever!*

It's clear from having viewed many thousands of home listings over the years that lots of agents don't do any real marketing whatsoever – to the detriment of their clients. Instead, they rely on two things to get the home *sold*: price, and luck. I'd rather not leave the success of your home sale up to either!

In the past 10-15 years, mobile phones, tablets, computers and the Internet have radically changed the way homes are *sold*. You may be having a hard time keeping up with all the technological "innovations" – and if so, you're on the same bus as a lot of real estate agents!

The way your home is presented on the Internet is today the #1 most important marketing aspect.

In my estimation, a large majority of agents simply have no clue about Internet marketing (which isn't too surprising, given the *average* age of a Realtor® is 58). Of course, there are a lot of great agents that are 58+ who are Internet savvy, and many of those who aren't can still do a fine job of selling your home. But today, if you have your choice, you'd be well advised to choose an agent with great Internet marketing chops.

And what about off-line sales and marketing? Many agents have no training whatsoever in copy writing, advertising, and basic sales skills such as answering the phone and lead follow-up. You'd think that their brokerage would train them – but few brokerages offer this kind of training. And even when a brokerage does provide it, it's rarely compulsory. Sadly, many agents simply don't see the value in this kind of training and will never avail themselves of it.

I don't want to paint all agents with a bad brush. But with real estate, as in any profession, most people are only so-so at their job. They do the minimum required to not get fired, and for most, that's good enough for them. And in a real estate brokerage, it's rare to get fired, unless an agent is serially unethical or criminal. Absent any push or enforced standards, few agents feel compelled to provide truly top-notch service.

Your average agent (and let's face it – most agents are pretty average!) uses what I call the Ron Popeil Marketing Plan. Perhaps you're familiar with it!

Most follow Ron Popeil's advice when it comes to marketing homes: they set it and forget it! They put it up on the MLS, stick a sign in the front yard, and forget all about it until the phone rings or an offer comes in. They might poke at it now and again by doing an open house or sending out an email blast, but that's pretty much it.

I developed my method over years of trial and error. While it continues to evolve, I feel that it is today the most thorough real estate marketing plan you'll ever come across. It's a process that I've used to list and sell hundreds of homes – and it will get yours *sold* too, faster and for more money. There are many components to my marketing plan, and here I've broken them into several categories.

Signpost Advertising

I don't just put a sign in your yard – I install a marketing-system-on-a-post! Here's what's included:

- **Dramatic Signage** - My signs are big and bold and jump right out at you. You can't miss 'em!
- **Prominent Phone Number** – Buyers won't have to hunt to find the number to call; it's easy to spot and will connect them with me directly.
- **Full Color Printed Flyers** – Great flyers are a very effective marketing tool. Mine have a QR code which allows buyers to quickly take a virtual tour of the home and get all the pertinent information any time. Except, *I leave the price off the flyers*, so people will usually connect with me to get it. This way, I have a better chance of getting them in the door for a private showing.

Yes, a sign in the yard is decidedly an old-school technique. And if your home is located down a quiet street that receives little or no traffic, the efficacy of a "for sale" sign is limited to announcing to buyers looking to drive by your home that they're at the right place.

Signposts are especially useful, however, when the home is located on any street that receives a decent amount of drive-by or walk-by traffic. Even in today's digital age, I receive many "sign calls" from buyers who hadn't seen the listing anywhere else. Don't discount this tried-and-true component of my marketing method.

Internet Marketing

> **Home Buyer Internet Statistics**
>
> - **97% of all buyers** used the Internet at some point in their home search
> - For 43% of recent buyers, **the first step that they took in the home buying process was to look online at properties for sale,** while 18% of buyers first contacted a real estate agent
> - 87% of homebuyers used a real estate agent
> - 51% of buyers in 2020 found their homes online
> - The typical buyer who used the Internet and searched for 8 weeks and visited 9 homes.
> - Among buyers who used the Internet during their home search, **89% of buyers found photos and 86% found detailed information about properties for sale very useful.**
> - 94% of buyers said they were very satisfied or somewhat satisfied with the home purchase process
>
> Source: NAR 2020 Profile of Home Buyers and Sellers

The statistics show that the Internet is the #1 way that buyers today search for homes, with 51% of buyers in 2020 having found the home they bought on the Internet. It's an indispensable part of the real estate search process. Your home needs to be *everywhere* on the Internet, so that wherever buyers are looking, your home is front and center. A first-class Internet marketing plan like mine has these elements:

> **Publication on Realtor® Websites** – Thanks to the "miracle" of syndication, the listing for your home will be found on all the most popular (and many not-so-popular!) real estate web sites. These include the national corporate sites of large brokerages like Compass and Redfin, and major franchises like Century 21, RE/MAX, Coldwell Banker, Keller Williams, and of course all the smaller

independent offices as well. If someone's a local Realtor® and they've got a web site, your home will be on it.

- **National Real Estate portals** – Of course, your listing will be seen on Zillow, Trulia, Realtor.com, Homes.com, HomeFinder, Movoto, HomeSnap and many more.
- **Craigslist** – Craigslist is a great place to find almost anything, including houses! While Craigslist real estate ads don't drive traffic like they used to, my Craigslist ads can still generate additional buyer inquiries.
- **Facebook Marketplace**: Craigslist has some stiff competition in the classified advertising space in the Facebook Marketplace. I list homes for sale there too and garner many responses for every home I post there.
- **Retargeting** – Have you ever looked to buy something on Amazon, and then seen an ad for that same product follow you around the Internet? That's called retargeting, and I do it with many of my listings. When someone sees your home on one of our sites, an ad for it will follow them around on the Internet and be seen on big-name web sites like the New York Times, CNN, Fox News, and thousands more.

I showcase my listings on 800+ web sites. Here are just a few...

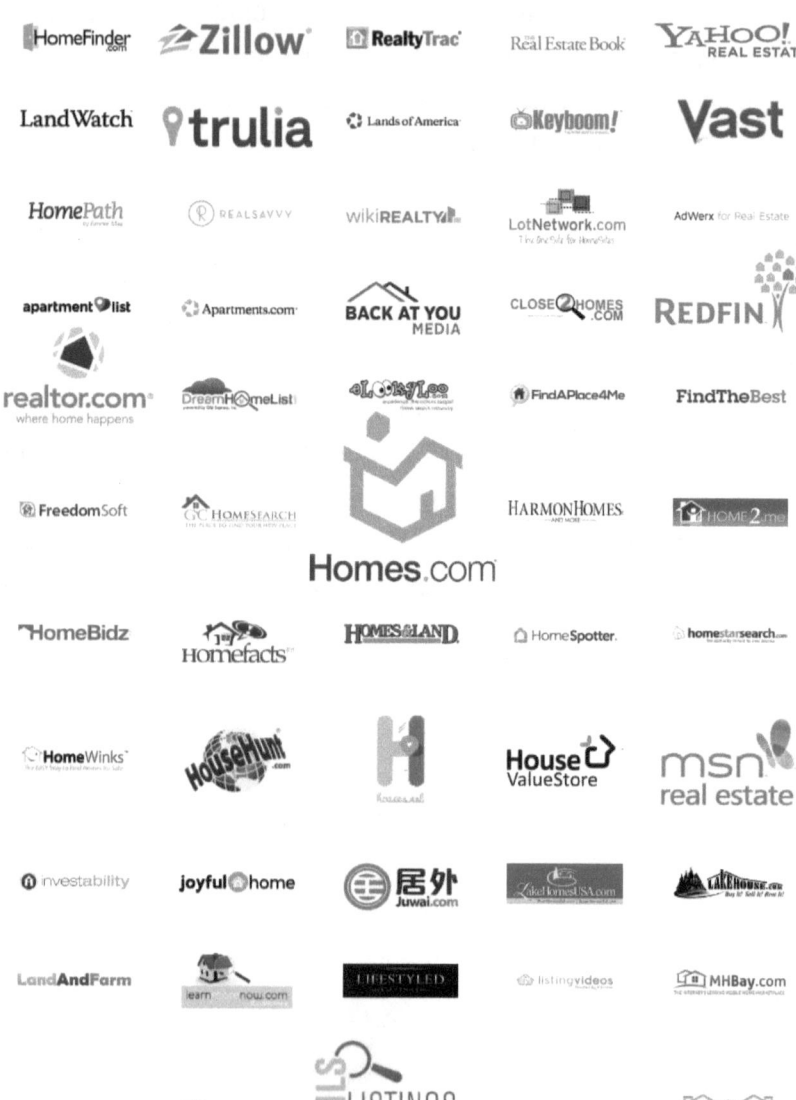

SebFrey.com

- **Search Engine Optimization** (SEO) – The systems I primarily use for sharing your home's listing on the web all use advanced search engine optimization techniques to make sure they rank highly on the Internet's most popular search engines.
- **Social Media** – Do I use Facebook? Check. Instagram? Pinterest? YouTube? LinkedIn? You betcha! I post my listings *everywhere*. I will of course share your listing with my 1500+ friends and followers on Facebook and Instagram, but I will also pay to advertise your listing to likely buyers on those platforms as well.

Print Advertising

- **Just Listed Cards** – I send postcards to your neighbors to make sure they know your home is for sale. Neighbors often know folks who want to move to the neighborhood.
- **Glossy Real Estate Magazines** – You've seen those glossy full-color real estate magazines at restaurants, coffee shops, and grocery stores, right? I may advertise your home there as well. This works best for more expensive listings that are likely to still be on the market when the magazine is finally printed and distributed.

UNSURPASSED MARKETING

- **Professional Photographs** – When it comes to getting your home *sold*, pictures are worth far more than a thousand words! In fact, having eye-popping pictures is key to getting the most interest in your property. A professional photographer shoots amazing photos on every one of my listings.

- **Virtual 3D Tour** - On listings where the technology is well suited, I employ 360° cameras to scan your home, to allow buyers to virtually walk through your home from the comfort of their smart phone, tablet, or computer.
- **Video presentation**– I will often create a custom video presentation for a home, which not only takes viewers through the home, but also showcases its features and benefits, as well as highlighting the neighborhood's amenities. After all, you're not just selling a home – you're selling a lifestyle, and video helps showcase it like nothing else.

- **Drone Video & Photography**– not all homes are good subjects for drones, but when they are a good fit for the technology, the results can be spectacular. Drone video and photography of the parcel, landscaping, and exterior of a home can add a feeling of drama, grandeur, and excitement in a way that terrestrial photography and video simply can't match.
- **Pre-Marketing** – I build anticipation and momentum for your listing through *pre-marketing* using a "Coming Soon" strategy. I advertise and make the home available to select buyers, brokers, and neighbors *before* the home is listed on the MLS. This allows the seller to get early feedback on the pricing and presentation before it gets wider public exposure, allowing for a fine-tuning of the marketing. It may also garner an offer before the home even hits the market! This is an essential step in my marketing plan, and I'll discuss it further below in the "Coming Soon" section.
- **Targeted Marketing** - For specific property types (e.g. horse property, farm homes, golf course homes, beach neighborhoods, vineyard homes) I will employ specialized targeted marketing when I know it will help attract a specific sort of buyer. I do this by purchasing a targeted list from data aggregators and uploading it to Facebook and Google as a "custom audience" and "customer list" respectively. It's tremendously effective at getttng the *right* buyers to see your home!
- **Love Letter and Features + Benefits** – I craft a "love letter" for every home from the seller, which extolls the joy of owning the home, what makes it a special place to live and to own. I also write up all the home's features and their

- *advantages*, so buyers understand a home's full value proposition.
- **The Party!** – Ever watch those *Million Dollar Listing* TV shows on Bravo? If so, you've probably noticed the *faaabulous* parties the agents throw for an open house or Broker's Tour. For select listings, and with the owner's permission and cooperation, I put on a fun event and invite your neighbors, other brokers, and my entire database to your place for a little fiesta and to see what your home has on offer.

Peer Marketing

Love 'em or hate 'em, we Realtors® do have at least one thing going for us: we're organized, and we help get each other's listings *sold*. I'm deeply involved with the local brokerage community, and I know I can count on my peers to help find the right buyers for my clients' homes.

- **My local brokerage community is working for you**. It's true. I personally and directly email all the local brokers about your listing and invite them and their buyers to the open houses, broker's tours, and any pre-marketing events. It sounds simple, but not many agents do it, and it gets attention. I also attend the local board's weekly Tour Meeting to tout your listing to my colleagues in the industry.
- **Thousands of MLS members work for you too**. I personally reach out to MLS member agents who I know have buyers for your home. It's called *reverse prospecting*. The MLS tells me which agents have clients that have searches set up that match your home's characteristics. I reach out to

these agents individually to make sure they've brought your home to their client's attention!

I'm always looking for new and innovative ways to market your home. Technology changes quickly, it could very well be that by the time you read this, I'll already have added new tools to my marketing toolbox. And I'm open to suggestions!

Coming Soon Strategy

Have you ever been to the movies? I'm guessing you have. You've probably noticed how a major motion picture doesn't suddenly appear on a theater marquee. Rather, Hollywood studios *pre-market* their productions for weeks, and in many cases months, before the theatrical release.

Why do they do that? They want to build excitement. Anticipation. Buzz. And, most importantly, they want to make sure there's throngs of people waiting to get into the theater when the curtain finally goes up.

And it's not just Hollywood that does it. Automakers do it. Book publishers do it. The music labels do it. Apple does it. Countless online marketers do it. And it turns out, it works exceptionally well for real estate sales too.

My coming soon strategy revolves around building a list of interested buyers (and agents with buyers) in the weeks before a home hits the market. Doing so primes the pump and assures you that from the word go you have buyers at the door and offers in hand shortly after that.

The numbers bear this out. Statistics have shown that homes with an effective "coming soon" strategy will sell faster, and sell for higher prices, than homes that do not. Compass, a nationwide real estate brokerage (and the dominant brokerage in Silicon Valley) states that their "Coming Soon" listings experience 2-3x more online views, enjoy 19% higher attendance at open houses, sell 7% faster, and for a sale price that is 1.74% higher compared to those homes which do not utilize this strategy. 1.74% might not sound like a lot more money, but that's $17,400 on a $1 million sale price. That's nothing to sneeze at in my book.

ACCEPTING AN OFFER WHILE "COMING SOON"

One important question that arises from the "coming soon" strategy is: what happens if you get an offer before your home hits the market? Should you consider accepting that offer before you've really exposed your home to all comers?

I believe that, generally speaking, the "coming soon" strategy is very useful to fill the pipeline of prospective purchasers and to get early feedback on pricing and presentation before you hit the open market. However, I do believe in caution when it comes to accepting an offer in the pre-marketing period.

I only recommend accepting a preemptive offer if it meets all of the seller's objectives with the terms and timing, <u>and comfortably exceeds what the seller could reasonably expect to see it sell for on the open market</u>, given the current market dynamics.

Even then, I'd be hesitant to accept any offer before a listing has been exposed to the open market. If the buyer who submits a pre-emptive offer really wants your home, they'll wait another few days for it to hit the market and for you to see if there's any competing offers. It's possible that you might end up getting lower offers, but I always advise clients to play by the numbers. The numbers say you'll get more money by having your home on the open market and taking offers from *all* prospective purchasers.

6
The Price is Right

Today's real estate buyers are savvy and empowered like never before. While the Internet has greatly increased the visibility of homes on the market, it has also provided greater access to data home buyers may not have had in years gone by.

It is now easier than ever for buyers to see which homes are up for sale and do a great deal of research on them in minutes, anytime, anywhere on their laptop, smartphone, or tablet. They know what's selling and for how much. You can't fool them. **Buyers today won't pay more for a property than they could for another, similar home which *appears* to offer the same value.**

Home buyers today are smart shoppers. Not only can homebuyers see what's for sale, they can also easily find out what homes have recently **sold** for. Since consumers now have access to this information, they have a better feel for home values - and overpricing a home means it's even *less* likely today than in the past that buyers will want to come to check out an overpriced home in person.

How can you as a seller take advantage of this environment, where buyers are so much more educated than they were before? The answer is that <u>most sellers are not as educated as buyers are today</u>, and a seller who *is* educated can exploit this information disparity.

It should come as no surprise that there are many overpriced homes on the market. If you regularly peruse real estate listings, you can't miss them – because they're the homes that keep showing up when you look. The right-priced homes will come and go, but the overpriced homes will stick out like a sore thumb.

It turns out, there's actually a reason that sellers tend to overprice their homes, and it's called the **Endowment Effect**. Richard Thaler, a professor of behavioral economics at the University of Chicago, coined the term for it (and won a Nobel Prize for his research). His research showed that humans – and primates, too – place more value on items that they own, compared to (nearly) identical items which they do not. Apparently, overvaluing things we possess has to do with a primal fear of loss, and that is certainly a tough one to overcome.

Nevertheless, that fear *can* be overcome! A smart seller will carefully review the market data and stuff down that fear to make a well-informed decision as to the list price. With faith in a trusted professional's guidance, they'll be able to set a price for their home which they can see will cause the home to sell, while other homes languish on the market.

I know that overcoming a primal fear is much easier said than done – but it can be done, especially if you fight fear with a good understanding of your local real estate market's dynamics, and some basic economic principles (which we'll discuss a little bit later on).

THE OPTIMAL LIST PRICE

I have performed literally thousands of home price evaluations over the years, in all kinds of markets, for the full spectrum of the housing stock. My experience has led me to conclude that estimating a home's sale price is a delicate blend of art and math. This is because no two homes are exactly the same. <u>No mathematical formula can 100% accurately determine what some unknown person will pay for a specific home several weeks or months in the future.</u> If such a formula did exist, someone would be making billions of dollars from the banks, gutting the appraisal industry.

The great thing about opinions is that everyone's got one – and you are certainly entitled to yours. But when it comes to opinions about home prices, you need to pay close attention to the facts, and the facts in this case are the *genuine* comparable sales. Sellers need to examine the *best* comps to dispassionately determine an asking price that will drive the right buyers to the home and yield the best offers.

Homeowners also need to be conscious of the fact that home prices don't stand still. Understanding how the market is trending (staying flat – or moving up or down, and at what velocity) plays a very important part in setting the optimal list price.

Pricing: What matters, and what doesn't

It's important to realize what matters and what doesn't in pricing your home. An area where homeowners get into trouble is that their opinion of their home's value - or what price they think someone will pay for it - is colored by factors which have nothing to do whatsoever with how much they can sell it for in the present market.

These factors include how much they paid for the home, how much they need to get when they sell the home, or how much money they have spent upgrading the home.

In an episode of *Million Dollar Listing* New York, Realtor® extraordinaire Fredrik Eklund tells his client something like: "I paid $2,000 for this suit. Are you going to buy it from me for $2,000?" The answer is no, obviously not. That suit is perhaps worth $2,000 to Frederick, but what's it worth to someone else?

Even if you could find someone else for whom the suit is a good-enough fit, they might be willing to pay only a couple hundred bucks for a second-hand suit - even if it did cost $2,000 not long ago and was worn by *the* Fredrik Eklund. The same is true for virtually every aspect of your home. You know what it's worth to you, but *what's it worth to someone else?*

That is the question, and it needs to be answered objectively. Remember: in most cases, buyers have options. They're not just looking at your home - they're looking at lots of homes. They are comparing your home to others, and looking at price, condition, location, and a whole host of other factors before they decide if they even want to drive by your home, much less go inside and then maybe write an offer on it.

Automated Pricing Systems

In the quest to come up with an easy and instant home price estimate, plenty of sellers visit web sites for online real estate price evaluations. They use popular web sites such as Zillow, Trulia,

Redfin, eppraisal.com and others, often with less than satisfactory results.

That these automated valuation web sites often get it wrong shouldn't be much of a surprise. There are so many factors going into a home's price, and these computer systems can't be expected to properly account for even a fraction of them, in every market across the country.

The algorithms used by these sites to calculate any property's value are proprietary and confidential, so nobody outside of these companies knows how exactly and for certain how they work. But it is generally believed that home valuation sites contract with major data aggregators such as Core Logic to obtain county tax roll data (all property is registered with the county for taxation purposes). They also find ways to become members of local multiple listing services (MLS), so they have access to listing data as well as historical sales data.

Between taxation and listing data, home valuation sites apply their own secret sauce (a computer algorithm) to come up with a "Zestimate" or an approximate price of what a home is likely to sell for. Sometimes, the results are spot on – because you know the saying: *even a broken clock is right twice per day*.

If you think about it though, you'll realize there's no way they can produce an estimate of value anyone should rely on. The algorithms can't (yet) consider whether a home has been updated, how well it's maintained, smell and cleanliness, or amorphous values such as a well-designed and functional floor plan, curb appeal, the appearance of other homes on the street, views, and so much more. For that reason, online valuations should be used only as one of several methods to estimate a home's value.

As Zillow says on its web site:

*"...the Zestimate is a good starting point as well as a historical reference, but **it should not be used for pricing a home.**"*

These sites are fun to play around on, but if you *really* want to know what your home is likely to sell for, hire an appraiser or ask a real estate professional for a customized home price analysis (more on that in a bit).

> **NOTE!**
> For a fresh take on automated home price web sites, visit SellForSure.com/homevalues This site includes a valuation from Realtor Property Resource, one of the best sources of automated valuations available today.

How Price is Determined

No matter what the *asking* price is for a home, in the end, *market* price is set by what one specific buyer is willing to pay. It's something of a neat trick to figure out how much an as-yet unidentified person will pay for your home, weeks or months ahead of time. However, through careful analysis of recent sales and market trends, I can calculate a narrow and realistic range of prices within which your home will sell.

To do this, I sift through all available sales data to discern the prices buyers have recently paid for homes in your neighborhood *that offer similar value*. Likewise, I check the listing prices of the homes which would meet the same needs as your buyer would have, *even if they are in a different neighborhood*. I'll look too and see what didn't sell – those listings which were withdrawn from the market or expired or canceled. From the data, I will create a custom home price analysis, called a CMA.

The CMA (Comparative Market Analysis)

An appraiser uses three methods to determine the value of your home: the replacement cost approach, the income approach, and the sales comparison approach.

The replacement cost approach values a property based on the land value, plus what it would cost to replace the building(s), minus depreciation. The income approach values a property based on the property's net operating income. The sales comparison approach values property based on the sale prices of similar properties in the area that have recently sold.

Appraisers reconcile all these approaches in their appraisal reports, but for most residential properties, they rely primarily on the sales comparison method to arrive at their valuation. This is because comparing your home to nearby, recent sales as well as homes presently listed for sale is the time-tested and truest way to determine how much someone is likely to pay for a home.

When seeking to calculate a home's likely sale price, I use a methodology similar to an appraiser. My CMAs will include homes recently *sold*, homes presently for sale, and, when relevant, homes which were on the market but did not end up selling (those where the listings expired, canceled, or were withdrawn from the market).

As I said earlier, pricing homes is a blend of art and math. To get the most accurate valuation, a real estate broker relies on his experience to select just the right "comps" that are overall most like your own home. <u>Any suggested price derived from a CMA is just the opinion of the preparer but should be well supported by the selected comparable properties.</u>

Picking the right comps is both a skill and an art. You don't want to trust this process to an unskilled agent, and you *definitely* shouldn't completely trust one of those automated valuation web sites that spit out a price based on a strict mathematical formula.

I've got to be honest here though: when I'm preparing a CMA, I *do* check those sites. I check Zillow, Redfin, Realtor.com, and ComeHome.com, to name a few. If these sites are so worthless, why do I check them? I check them because I know my clients are checking them, and the valuations they provide are part of the conversation. It's also interesting to note just how far apart in pricing these automated "intelligent" systems usually are.

I've been selling real estate now for over 18 years, and in that time, I've been inside lots of houses, in many different neighborhoods. I've seen, listed, and *sold* them all from tumbledown backwoods shacks to shabby chic beachfront homes, and everything in between. Over time, I've honed a sense for what adds to (or subtracts from) the value of a home in my market.

Not only do I have many years of experience in my local housing market, I am to this day actively involved in the thick of it. With each passing week, I become more in tune with its nuances, the ebb and flow of homes and buyers, and I share this wealth of knowledge with my clients.

To complement my rich and varied "field experience," I use several advanced software tools to aid me in the process of providing what I consider to be the most accurate pricing data on your home. I examine the data through the lens of my years of experience, taking the following factors into primary consideration.

LOCATION

When researching for a CMA, I will strive to use comparable sales <u>from the immediate neighborhood</u>. But I don't just look at the "comparables" – I look at *every* sale in the neighborhood, comparable or not, to get a feel for what buyers are paying the most for, what's moving and what's sitting.

When considering location, it's also important to consider comparable listings (not sales: actual current listings, especially those which are "pending sale") *in different neighborhoods*. Most buyers are not looking for homes exclusively in *your* neighborhood. They might *prefer* your neighborhood, but what do you want to bet there's another neighborhood or two they might *also* be happy with, if there's a home they love, and the price is right?

Because of this, I may include comparable properties in my CMA from nearby, rival neighborhoods as well, as these properties are very much working to attract the same buyers you are.

SQUARE FOOTAGE

I always want to keep the "comps" to within 300 square feet of the size of the "subject property." In many areas, this isn't possible as the housing stock can be so varied, but I do the best I can.

It's very important to choose comparables that are very close to the same square footage as the subject property I'm valuing. That's because the larger the home, the lower the price-per-square foot. Conversely, the smaller the home, the higher the price-per-square foot (all other factors being roughly equal).

LOT SIZE AND CHARACTERISTICS

I look to keep my comparable properties to within 10% of your home's lot size. After all, in California at least, the lion's share of your home's value is the dirt that's sitting underneath it. Any valuation of your home must pay special attention to both the lot size as well as overall lot utility and ease of access.

When considering lot size, it's important to understand too that the land value does not increase in direct proportion to its size – far from it. Appraisers use the term "excess land" when considering properties with oversize lots. They don't increase in value as much as you might think because the excess land isn't needed to serve or support the existing use, and often (due to zoning) cannot be repurposed for another higher and better use.

AGE

When it comes to age, I always try to find homes that were built within 10 years of the subject property. Due to the variety of housing stock in many areas, this may not be possible. Mind you, a home's *effective age* is also very important in determining value. If a home was built in 1960 but was taken down to the studs and completely remodeled in in the past year, most consumers will consider it – and pay for it – like it's a brand-new home.

BONUS AREAS

Areas like basements, high-ceilinged attics, detached studios and the like are also factors which drive prices. These bonus areas can have a substantial impact on a home's price, <u>especially if these spaces can be pressed into service as additional sleeping areas</u>.

They're called "bonus areas" because they are not typically recognized by the local building department as habitable areas, and so are not counted in square footage. Often times, the only heat source in these spaces comes from portable space heaters, although many homeowners will install baseboard heat or run a heating duct to them. Even though these spaces don't "legitimately" count as square footage, buyers do see value – often times, a lot of value – in them, and their presence needs to be accounted for in any valuation.

It's worthwhile noting that because these bonus areas aren't (usually) counted in the square footage, sites like Zillow won't take them into account when pricing a property.

CONDITION

The closer a home feels to new construction, the more value homebuyers will attribute to it. It's perceived as more modern, up to date, and less like a money pit. It should go without saying that homes that are not updated or in poor repair sell for less than otherwise similar homes. You'd be surprised, though: this is something that is often overlooked or underappreciated when selecting comparable properties, but it has a big impact on price. Pay close attention to the condition of the comparables and the subject property (the home you're estimating a price for). If a "comparable" property has a lavishly updated kitchen slathered in marble and peppered with German appliances, but yours has chipped Formica counters and worn linoleum flooring, you'll need to adjust your estimate accordingly.

This is an area where automated valuation sites like Zillow fall down flat. While Zillow is working on machine-learning algorithms that can, for example, recognize an upgraded kitchen from one built in the 1970s, I'm doubtful they'll ever get to the point where their algorithm will be able accurately price the *feeling* buyers get when walking through a home. After all, most buyers will pay only what they *feel* the home is worth, and no more.

LANDSCAPING AND OUTDOOR AMENITIES

Appraisers rarely make mention of the landscaping, but buyers sure pay attention to it. California has a Mediterranean climate, and much of the reason people are willing to pay big bucks for real estate here is due to the fabulous weather. A home's ability to provide high quality indoor-outdoor living is a major factor affecting home values, and it must receive proper consideration.

ADDITIONAL CONSIDERATIONS

There are many more things to think about when valuing a home, and what follows is only a partial list. These additional factors include the number of bedrooms, bathrooms, garage spaces, off-street parking, granny units, living areas, outbuildings, pools, views, proximity to employers, shopping, restaurants, entertainment, and recreation, school districts, and much more.

Review of each comparable

In my initial sweep of the data, I select a lot of properties for consideration. I'll carefully scrutinize the attributes of these homes, as well as the photographs and descriptions of each. I evaluate dozens of properties, one by one, and home in on just the few that are most indicative of what buyers will pay for a home like yours in the present market. I'll often drive through the neighborhood and get my eye on prospective comps for my report and will get inside the homes whenever possible.

It's tempting to want to include a *lot* of comps in a valuation report, because I know clients will ask about them. "Why didn't you include 123 Main Street, it's just around the corner and sold last month?" is something I'll frequently hear when going over these reports.

The best CMAs include just the *most relevant* comparable sales. My goal is to provide 3-4 recent sales, and 3-4 listed or "pending sale" homes, and a handful of expired / canceled / withdrawn listings when looking at them is useful.

One thing we're all drowning in today is information – it comes at you as if from a firehose, all day, every day. You hire a professional, like me, to analyze that information and distill it down to the most applicable information you need to focus on. That's what I seek to deliver with every CMA I produce for my clients.

Pricing Strategy Discussion

Once I've thoroughly analyzed all the data, and have had a chance to tour the property, the last step of the CMA process is the determination as to my suggested list price. This price is predicated on following my marketing plan; any significant deviation from the plan would alter my recommendation for the listing price.

Market values can fluctuate rapidly. Immediately prior to listing a home, the market should be evaluated, and the list price carefully calibrated to account for current market conditions.

The first part of any discussion about pricing needs to be about the marketing strategy, because pricing and marketing are intertwined. It's very important that clients understand how the marketing is intended to work, and that they're on board with the plan. After educating my clients about the intricacies of my marketing system, we move on to a discussion about price.

The list price is actually a pillar of the marketing plan. The list price is one of the first things people will notice about your property, so it all starts from there and what expectations buyers will have of a property with that price in that neighborhood.

Setting a high initial list price will necessarily alter the plan by requiring more expensive home preparation. A higher price will also mean attracting a different (usually smaller) buyer pool, which may increase your time on market. Vexingly, a longer time-on-market is strongly correlated with *lower* sales prices, so it's important that when setting a higher list price, you **don't set it *too* high**.

If there's one key take-away from this section of the book, it's this: <u>the price you set has more to do with how long you want to keep the home on the market, and not so much with what it will ultimately sell for, and that the longer a home is on the market, the less it's likely to sell for.</u>

That may seem counterintuitive, I get it. And it's not exactly a law of nature. If you wait long enough – years, maybe – and the market is rising, you may finally get your asking price. After years paying interest on a mortgage, insurance, and maintenance on a house you no longer want. Meanwhile, other asset and commodity prices will probably also have risen, putting into question if you really "made" more money at all.

Numerous studies have shown that homes which take longer to sell ultimately sell for less. Sure, some of these studies were bought and paid for by the National Association of Realtors, so I can see why you might take those with a grain of salt. I invite you to do some research – just Google something like "academic studies sale price vs time on market real estate." You will find a variety of studies which have shown this to be true.

Once my clients understand the role that pricing plays in the marketing plan and its impact on the actual sale price, we move on to review the market analysis (CMA) and my *proposed* list price. It's only a proposal; after I've helped my clients see how and why I came up with my suggestion, *I want my clients to choose the list price that **they** think will get them the best result based on their goals.*

That's right – <u>I always want my clients to set their own home's list price</u>. It's my job to show my clients what I think is the best way to quickly net them the most cash at closing (by following my marketing plan), and what I believe the market is saying about the likely sale price of their home, given my marketing methodology. From time to time, my clients will choose to have a higher price than I recommend – and that's fine. My job is to give them the information they need to make an informed decision, but the decision is theirs to make.

Once the seller has set the price, my job is then to do my utmost to get the home *sold* at the price the seller is asking, as swiftly as possible. It's only once I'm sure that the sellers have had their questions answered and are confident in both the marketing plan and the initial list price that we move on to writing up a listing agreement.

Want to Sell your House? Don't get Bought!

It's a sad fact: many home sellers make the unfortunate mistake of selecting whichever real estate agent tells them their home is worth the most. Most agents know this, so to secure your business they'll tell you they see your home selling for a *really high price.*

This is so common that there's actually a term for it: it's called "buying the listing." If you really want to get your house sold, my advice to you is: *don't get bought!*

It's fine to ask the agents you interview how much they think they can sell your house for. But remember: the agent isn't the one who's going to be buying your home. The agent's opinion ultimately matters much less than that of whoever plunks down the money and completes the purchase.

So, while it's **OK** to ask agents how much they think your house is worth, there's a more important question to ask. And that question needs to be asked of yourself.

That question is: which agent do I think can get me the very highest price for the property that the market will bear – *whatever that price may be?*

Nobody can tell you for sure, with 100% accuracy, exactly what your home will sell for. Pick the agent that *you* feel will do the best job of getting top dollar for your home, on your own terms.

Other Pricing Factors

ABSORPTION RATE

Is your market like a sponge?

The absorption rate measures how quickly homes on the market are being *sold* relative to the supply. Let's say there are 100 homes available for sale in your neighborhood and 10 are *sold* each month. If no new homes are listed, the entire supply of homes in your neighborhood would be absorbed in 10 months. If the market is absorbing properties slowly, and you need to sell quickly, you ought to price your home accordingly if you *need* it to sell within a particular timeframe.

THE COMPETITION

You might feel your home is worth a million dollars - but be conscious of the *Principle of Substitution*. If a buyer has $1,000,000 to spend on a home, are they going to buy your home, or buy the home six blocks over which is "pretty much the same" only it's 1,000 square feet bigger, on a double lot, in a better school district and is listed for "only" $949,000?

If you're asking $800,000 for your home, check into what else a buyer can get for that same $800,000 and honestly consider if your home is an equal (or superior) substitute for another which is also asking $800,000. If it's not, you'll need to re-examine your expectations for your home's sale price. No matter the situation, buyers always choose the home that appears to offer the best price, condition, and location for their money.

Remember, too, that in most cases, buyers are not just looking at homes in your neighborhood. While they might *prefer* your neighborhood, they're usually open to other neighborhoods as well. If they find a house they love for a price they'll pay in a competing neighborhood they're happy with, they'll probably buy that home if it appears to offer greater value for the price.

The Buyer's Appraisal

It's my sad duty to inform you that there's an "independent" third party who will pass judgement on whatever price you've agreed to with your buyer. Typically, around 15-25% of purchases are all cash, but the odds are your buyer will need a loan to buy your home. Naturally, a bank loan means an appraisal will be required (except under some limited circumstances).

> **NOTE!**
>
> When a buyer gets an FHA loan, they will also get an FHA appraisal. The FHA appraisal sticks with your property for six months. If the FHA buyer falls out of contract, and another FHA buyer comes along, that buyer will use the same FHA appraisal as the previous buyer.

If the appraiser says the home is worth less than the contract sale price, drama may ensue. In many cases, a low appraisal will result in the buyer's loan being declined. Even if the loan isn't declined, most buyers have an *appraisal contingency*, and if the house fails to appraise for the sale price, the buyer can cancel the contract – or, more likely, renegotiate the deal at a lower price. Appraisal issues are the second most frequent cause of broken deals (inspection issues are #1).

When reviewing an offer from a buyer, check to see if they're stipulating an appraisal contingency (they usually will, unless it's a cash offer). You should know though that with a big enough down payment, the buyer probably does not actually *need* an appraisal contingency.

That's because most loans require only that there be an 80% debt-to-equity ratio. For example, if the buyer is putting down $300K on a $1 million property, the loan amount is $700K. That means that if the property appraises for at least $875K ($700K is 80% of $875K), there won't be an issue with the lender because the debt-to-equity ratio meets loan guidelines.

If the buyer is asking for an appraisal contingency, but does not appear to need one, the seller should counter the buyer on this point. Of course, many buyers will be using all or most of their cash available for the down payment and purchase price, and they absolutely need the property to appraise at contract price, to maintain that 80-20 debt-to-equity ratio.

Therefore, it's important to do everything you can to make sure the buyer uses a lender that draws from an experienced appraisal pool who knows the local neighborhoods and housing stock. This lessens the chance of an out-of-area appraiser killing the deal with a low appraisal.

> Like a CMA, an appraisal is just one man's opinion of value. Indeed, the Uniform Appraisal Report used for a buyer's loan will state:
>
> "The purpose of this summary appraisal report is to provide the lender/client with an accurate, and adequately supported, *opinion* of the market value of the subject property." (emphass added)

Pricing Unique and Luxury Properties

Your home is your castle – and for some people, that is literally true! In the case of homes which are rare, unusual, and have unique characteristics and attributes such as you'd find in upper-end luxury homes, it's not a bad idea to pay for a formal appraisal report. For  properties like this, the alternative approaches used for valuation (replacement cost and income) may be given more weight and can lead to a more accurate valuation. An appraisal will still be just one person's opinion, but buyers will view it as a very credible data point which supports your asking price.

Having a recent appraisal available for marketing purposes on distinctive and unusual properties can be a big plus. This is especially true if you're willing to list it for a price at something of a discount off the full appraised value. This provides "proof" to the buying public that your home is in fact priced to sell and a very good value.

Pricing Strategies

AS-IS PRICING STRATEGY

The fact is most homes in California are *sold* on an "as-is" basis – that's how the standard California Residential purchase agreement we Realtors® use is written (I'll discuss what "as-is" means in the purchase contract in greater detail later on).

However, using the term "as-is" in a pricing (marketing) strategy tells the buyers that the home has a few things that need fixing, and that *the asking price takes that into consideration*. Depending on your "most likely" buyer, this may be a good strategy, because some folks are looking for a home that will allow them to build "sweat equity."

"MOVE-IN READY" PRICING STRATEGY

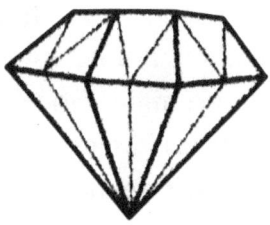

This is the opposite of the "as-is" pricing strategy. You can do this with homes that are in pristine, "everything's been done" condition. Of course, you'll provide the inspection reports which show that the property is (largely) free of defects and significant needed repairs

To back up the message of quality and hassle-free ownership, you can offer the buyer an upgraded two-year home warranty with their full price offer. While some buyers are looking for an "as-is" fixer-upper, many *more* buyers strongly prefer "move-in ready" homes and will pay a premium for them.

OVERPRICING "STRATEGY"

In any discussion on pricing strategies, we need to talk about the phenomena of overpricing your home for sale. Overpricing is an ill-advised but all-to-common phenomena where a homeowner inexplicably decides to put their home up for sale with a price that is considerably more than anyone is likely to pay for it.

NOTE! Overpricing a home is risky! Studies have repeatedly shown that the longer a property stays on the market, the greater the discount for the buyer.

Sometimes this is done on accident, but many times it is done intentionally. When done on purpose, the twisted "logic" used to justify overpricing is that this will leave room to negotiate. The thinking goes that buyers can always offer less, and the price can be reduced later if need be.

I believe there are two main factors which cause homeowners to intentionally overprice their home. The first is when they aren't in a rush to sell. If they have no specific date by which they need to sell their home, many homeowners will feel more comfortable setting a higher price for their home. Buyers pick up on this though; they'll get a sense that a seller doesn't *really* want to sell and will hold back on making an offer.

The second main reason homeowners tend to set a high price is when their home is unique - unique to the point where there may be few buyers for it, or where there is a lack of good comparable sales data to show what the price should be. In cases like this, when the property is much less of a commodity for which traditional rules of economics are less applicable, overpricing a home *may* make some sense.

For homes with unique characteristics and amenities, buyers will tend to focus first on these attributes of the home, rather than the price. It's for this reason that high end luxury homes tend to sell for substantially less than asking price. Buyers for these homes are not shopping in a price range per se, they're looking for just the right property, and will negotiate as required once they find it.

An important thing to consider, though, is that things which *you* may love about your home that make it unique are things which most buyers won't appreciate. Many buyers look at these unique characteristics as things to remove or replace. In other words, these characteristics are often times net-negatives, and reduce the value people see in your home (and lower the price they'd be willing to pay).

The reality is though that while every home is in fact unique, most homes are better thought of as commodities. They're similar enough to other homes that buyers can get a good read on what a fair price is. In most cases, your home is not as unique as you might think it is, and you'll suffer in more ways than one by overpricing it.

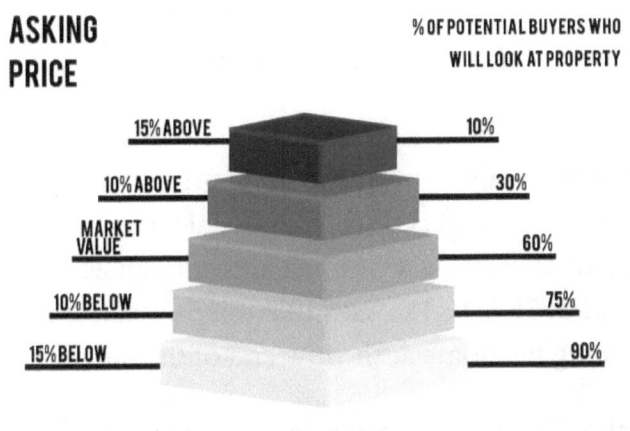

If buyers feel the price you're asking is too far off from their sense of fair market value, they'll simply move on, and make an offer on another property for sale. In most cases, <u>overpricing your home only serves to help sell competing homes in your market area</u>. It has the effect of extending your time on market, and in many cases, it reduces the ultimate sale price of your home below what you would have received had you priced the home correctly at the outset.

The Virtue of Underpricing your Home

Underprice my home you say? Typical Realtor®, you're thinking. But hear me out here, please! There's method to my madness, and sound economic principles, too.

For some homes - especially newer tract homes in a subdivision full of very similar homes - it's going to be pretty clear what the market price of the home is, given its condition. If that's clear, then go ahead and list it at that price, and expect that you'll get full asking price. If the price is clear to you, it out to be clear to other buyers as well - which is why it's an *especially* bad idea to over-price a home in a neighborhood with a good selection of very similar homes.

However, many homes are in older, established neighborhoods where prices are really all over the map. Given all the factors that go into determining market price, it's possible that you'll figure your home is worth something within a range of values - say between $500,000 and $525,000. In cases like this, a seller might want to consider pricing the home at the low end of the range.

Why's that? Because the economic principal called *price elasticity of demand* will work in your favor. It's simple: *demand for goods like real estate is elastic relative to its price*. That is, when the price gets lower, demand gets higher. Some goods are inelastic, and the demand for them will not change much with fluctuations in price (think food, toilet paper, and many other essential commodities).

It turns out though that real estate is a product that *does* experience considerable elasticity of demand. When the price is lower, demand is much stronger. Stronger demand shows up in the form of more inquiries, showings, open house visitors, and multiple offers. Multiple offers almost invariably lead to a sale price over asking price – sometimes a *lot* over asking.

Bear in mind that by listing a home for sale, <u>you are not obligated to accept an offer at list price</u>. Listing a home is merely an invitation to submit offers. If you list your home for what you consider is a low price, and only get offers at that price, you are not required by law to accept the offer. You are perfectly within the law to counter the offer at a higher price, or outright reject it.

But if you've *truly* underpriced your property, that is, listed it for sale slightly below "market price," whatever that happens to be – buyers *will* recognize that, and *market forces* will work in your favor. You'll get offers, and plenty of them, and it's very common to see sale prices jump into nosebleed territory. You go from worrying "Did I price it too cheap?" to "Wow, do you think it will appraise for that much?"

I get that trusting in the unseen hand of the market is tough to do. You're Han Solo and you're not buying this whole bit about some mysterious "force." But when it comes to pricing, I'm a Jedi Master, and you'd do well to heed my advice on this one.

7
Preparing your Home For the Market

Ever buy a used car? Used car dealers can spend thousands of dollars repairing and detailing cars prior to resale. This is one way they can command such high prices for their vehicles. They create value in the minds of buyers by making their vehicles look sharp – as close to "new" as possible. It's one reason you can save so much money buying a car from a private party on Craigslist, because many private vehicle sellers just put their cars up for sale with no thought to the presentation.

The same principle applies to selling your home. The closer you get your home to looking "like new", the more demand (and more dollars) you'll receive for your home. Home buyers just *love* new construction (even if a lot of homes built these days are practically just made from cardboard).

If it helps, think of it as a beauty contest, where looks *really* matter. Looks aren't *all* that matter, but it is perhaps at the top of the list. If you want your home to sell for a million bucks – your home better *look* like a million bucks. Most buyers will not be fooled by lipstick on a pig, but they will respond very favorably to a home that is clean, coiffed, and poised to strut on the runway.

Helping a seller make their home show in the best possible light is one of my most important jobs a real estate broker. What's possible will vary considerably, given the time and resources available. But when it comes to selling a home, I always remember the timeless words of Abraham Lincoln: "Give me six hours to chop down a tree and I will spend the first four sharpening the axe."

When you set about the work of preparing your home for sale, you need to detach yourself from your home and make an *objective* survey of its condition. You'll be aided in your assessment by doing pre-sale inspections, and consultation from a professional home stager will show you what cosmetic items should be addressed (more on that later).

If you'll still be living in your home while it's on the market, you need to strike a very delicate balance between best staging practices and your need to keep living your life. I don't know too many folks that keep their favorite furniture stacked up in the garage, never leave a dirty dish in the sink, and keep the dining room table perpetually set with formal place settings morning, noon, and night. There's a reason why you don't too often see *people* on the pages of *Sunset* or *Dwell* magazine! People are messy, but when you're selling a home, it should not be.

Just remember that <u>the way you live in a home, and the way you sell a home, are usually two completely different things</u>. You may feel it isn't your home if you're living in it during the sale process, and in a way, it won't be. After all, you're making a transition from it being your home, to its being someone *else's* home.

You'll recall from chapter 3 that there are four major factors in a successful sale of a home: marketing, pricing, negotiation, and *preparation*. In fact, the way you prepare your home for market usually has more to do with how much money you'll ultimately get when the home is **sold** than any other factor. That's why it it's so important to get this part of the sale process right.

While this stage of the sale is critical, I always seek to minimize the cash outlay to the greatest degree possible. I aim to have whatever money you *do* spend give you a 2-5x return on the cost upon sale. This will be money very well spent – or, rather, invested.

During my initial consultation, one of the first questions I ask my clients is how much money they can afford to invest in their home getting it ready for sale. Once I know how much money we have to work with, I prioritize the work based on how much I expect it will improve their bottom line.

I find that on average, sellers spend 1-3% of the sale price on pre-sale preparations. Some spend less, some spend more – it depends on the condition of the home and the seller's appetite for getting the work done. But if you need to spend $10,000 to get a $20,000-$50,000 return in just a few months, any financial advisor will tell you that's an excellent use of capital.

WHY PREPARATION IS PROFITABLE

Over the years, I've had many people question the value of putting money into their homes before putting it on the market. There is, shall we say, a healthy skepticism that doing simple things like painting, landscaping, upgrading the lighting and plumbing fixtures, can have that much of an impact on a home's resale value.

Many people accept that they can get a dollar-for-dollar return, but don't see how they're going to get 2-5x return on their money, as I'm suggesting is possible here in this book. After all, why would a buyer pay $30,000 for a $10,000 paint job?

There are a number of reasons for this. The market's appetite for *move-in ready homes* is much greater today than in the past (although there's always been plenty of appetite for them). When I began my career in real estate sales in 2003, it seemed that everyone wanted a fixer upper. Now, it seems that *nobody* wants a fixer upper (except flippers). Who has the time for all that? It seems like everyone's working all day, every day, and people just want a home they can buy, fill it with their furnishings, and get right on living. That's what most people want, and they'll pay a premium for it.

And there's not only the time and effort it would require of the buyer to do this work. There's also the question of the *money*. Most buyers aren't paying cash. In fact, according to the 2020 NAR Profile of Home Buyers and Sellers, the average down payment amount in 2020 was 12% among all buyers. Most buyers are not going to have a lot of cash left over to do the work your home may need after closing.

When buyers choose a home that's already had the work done, they are in effect rolling the cost of that work into their loan. Real estate mortgages have exceptionally low interest rates – at the time of writing, they're averaging around 2.75%. But even at 3.5%, 4.5% or more, it's still much cheaper than any other consumer credit they might use to pay for work on the property.

Interested in something less anecdotal? Appraisers have a term which describes all of this: *Entrepreneurial Profit*. It's the reason why house flippers and home builders are able to make the money they do. To quote from *The Appraisal of Real Estate* (12th edition), Entrepreneurial Profit is:

> A market derived figure that represents the amount an entrepreneur receives for his or her contribution to a project and risk; the difference between the total cost of a property (cost of development) and its market value (property value after completion), which represents the entrepreneur's compensation for the risk and expertise associated with development.

In this case, you – the homeowner – are the entrepreneur. Should you decide to sell your home without doing the work which would bring up its market value, you make your *buyer* the entrepreneur who can then improve the home's value by doing that work.

The amount of entrepreneurial profit to be made from, say, painting a house will vary from time to time and market to market. I've experienced markets where a paint job might only return double the cost; other times, I've seen it easily return 5x.

When deciding on what work you want to do preparing your home for sale, you should work closely with a Realtor® to make sure that the juice is worth the squeeze. Not everything you *could* do to your home will boost its value, and depending on the cost, could barely break even, or even be a net loss to you.

Even when I show my clients how and why these pre-sale improvements and renovations can significantly improve their bottom line, many homeowners are still hesitant to do the work. One of the biggest reasons is getting the money to pay for it. I cover that in the "Creative Ways to Pay for Home Preparation" section later in this book. The other big thing stopping them is the *hassle* and their inexperience with doing this kind of work on their homes.

It's for this reason that top-notch Realtors like myself offer what I call *Concierge Services*.

Concierge Services

Let's face it: selling a home is a big project. It's probably one reason you've put off selling as long as you have. Like I said earlier: who's got the time? I take helping sellers one step further, by offering what I call *Concierge Services*.

When I'm selected as the listing agent, I manage the entire sale process for my clients, from the moment they sign a listing agreement, and every step of the way until you get your check with the proceeds of the sale. It's a "done for you" experience which is second to none.

Here are just some of the services I manage for my clients:

- Public records research
- Inspections
- Cleaning
- Trash / debris disposal
- Repair recommendations
- Obtain competing bids from contractors
- Overseeing repairs
- Landscaping
- Painting
- Flooring
- Staging
- Escrow coordination
- Buyer and lender vetting
- Personal organizing
- Packing

- Moving

Of course, I don't do it alone, I bring in a team. Working with the best stagers, inspectors, contractors, handymen and landscapers, I figure out what needs to be done inexpensively and cost-effectively to get you the very highest price for your home.

The Fabulous Four - Preparation Tasks

When it comes to selling your home for top dollar, there are four tasks (the "fab four!") which cost the least and, happily, provide *by far* the biggest bang for the buck. These key tasks are **de-cluttering, landscaping, cleaning, and painting.**

1. **De-clutter.** Over the years we stuff our homes with a lot of furniture, knick-knacks, artwork, equipment toys, books – all kinds of junk. I'm here to tell you, *it's all gotta go!* Well, not *all* of it – but a very large portion of it needs to disappear.

When it comes to de-cluttering, think big, open, and clear sight lines. You want to maximize floor and counter space. A professional stager will make good recommendations on which pieces of furniture should be removed, and where the remaining pieces should be distributed. In the kitchen and bathrooms, you'll want to stash away appliances, personal care products, and anything else which makes the room look busy.

Part of de-cluttering also means de-personalizing. You don't want buyers looking at your *stuff*. Take down family photos, mementos, your kid's artwork – anything that makes it look like *your* home. You want the buyer to feel like your house is a clean slate where they can write the next chapter of *their* lives in big bold print.

2. **Clean**. Once you've removed the clutter, a thorough deep cleaning is essential. This means scrubbing down your home, from top to bottom, inside and out. *Pay particular attention to the kitchen and bathrooms; these must be spotless!* Don't let anything escape the sponge, brush, or mop. Clean all the way from the spider webs near the ceiling to the dust bunnies in the corners of the floor. The exterior of your home, decks, patios, walkways, and the driveway should be power washed.

Your home may already be immaculate, in which case, you're already done with the cleaning part! However, I've found that most homes could use a thorough scrubbing. I suggest that you form a cleaning crew, made up of your family and some friends if they'll help – throw in some pizza and beer and you might get a whole army of volunteers! If you have more money than time, a professional cleaning crew will typically cost $300-$600 depending on the size and grunginess of your home.

3. **Paint**. After you've removed a lot of furnishings and de-personalized by taking down photographs and family artwork, you'll find that painting your home is going to be a lot easier than if you had to navigate around all that *stuff*. It could be you just need to do some touch-ups, but *unless you've painted within the last couple of years, nothing beats a whole fresh coat of paint*. At $35-$40 per gallon, fresh paint and your own elbow grease is a bargain-basement way to boost the sale price of your home (so long as you do a decent job of it, of course).

4. **Landscaping.** The way your home looks when buyers drive by, pull up, and get out of their cars is crucial. If people don't like what they see from the curb, they may just drive away. Trim trees, bushes, and grass. Add new plants and flowers to add some visual "pop". Drive around your neighborhood and see which houses have the most appealing yards and copy those design elements where you can. Don't neglect the back yard, either – the front yard is crucial, but if your back yard is a mess, clean it up, trim it back, and make it look as cultivated as possible.

Landscaping is something many people can do on their own, or if you need to hire it out, it is among the lowest-cost jobs you can pay someone to do.

Home Repairs

You might already have a "honey-do" list of things you've been meaning to fix around the house – now that you're selling, there's no better time than now to tackle these chores! I've got a little bad news for you though – your list is about to get a lot longer. You'll probably end up adding all kinds of things like replacing damaged or out-of-style light fixtures, replacing light bulbs with those with higher wattage, replacing torn window and screens, re-caulking in the kitchen and bathrooms, taking care of leaking faucets, cracked windows, loose doorknobs, and much more.

The foundation could use a little work...

A lot of this stuff probably seems like small beer and not worth bothering about, but trust me – left unresolved, these kinds of things can raise a red flag. Home buyers will get a *feeling* that the home has not been well cared for and that it's going to need a lot of work on their part if they buy it. Remember: getting the highest price for your home means creating an *emotional connection* with your buyer, so how buyers *feel* about your home is of utmost importance.

You can probably go around the house yourself and make a list of things that need fixing – or you can let the home and termite inspectors do it for you. Create a list of fixes from their reports, and then add in the cosmetic recommendations from the home stager. You're likely to wind up with a list of *dozens* of discrete items. A good real estate broker (like myself!) can recommend contractors and handymen to take care of these items quickly and at the best prices in the area.

DIY Home Repair Tips

Some people are just very hands on and want to tackle repairs before they call out any inspectors or other professionals to look their homes over. For folks like that, I've compiled a list here of the most common types of repairs that people make on their homes prior to putting them on the market.

- ➢ Repair leaking faucets, running toilets, grout, and caulking as needed.
- ➢ Replace any cracked windows and torn screens.
- ➢ Patch and paint wall and ceiling cracks (but disclose that you have done this!)

- Repair or replace loose or corroded doorknobs and hinges.
- Make sure drawers, windows, and doors open smoothly.
- Install any missing towel racks, switch plates, and outlet covers.
- Tack down any loose molding and glue down any lifted wallpaper (or better yet – ditch the wallpaper!).
- Have the furnace cleaned and inspected if you haven't done it in over a year and make the inspection report available to buyers.
- If you have an automatic garage door opener – make sure it works smoothly.

Point of Sale Retrofits and Inspections

When real property is transferred in California, there may be some government-mandated retrofits or inspections required of your home. These are called "point of sale" ordinances and they vary among jurisdictions.

These are usually minor, and include installation of smoke and carbon monoxide detectors, and that the water heater(s) be seismically strapped. Smoke and Carbon Monoxide detectors are inexpensive and can be had for as low as $10 apiece - or even less if you buy them in bulk. Seismic strapping might cost up to $125 for parts and labor installed by a contractor, or considerably less than that if you do it yourself.

Depending on the location of your property, the local government may require that the toilets and shower heads be low-flow fixtures. The shower heads are very inexpensive and not a concern; many toilets run about $250-$300 apiece, installed. Fortunately, many municipal water utilities offer rebates when you install these low-flow fixtures, so be sure to check with your water company.

Unfortunately, not all "point of sale" retrofits are as inexpensive as these. Many parts of California are now mandating that the sewer laterals meet a certain standard upon sale. A "sewer lateral" is the pipe that runs from the home to the main sewer line in the street. Bringing a sewer lateral into compliance can be expensive, with costs sometimes soaring into the tens of thousands of dollars.

The standard California Residential Purchase Agreement has boxes to check specifying if the buyer or seller is to pay for these retrofits. Typically, the seller is expected to pay for them, however, it is negotiable. As these costs can be considerable, a smart seller will know what these costs are likely to be before going into contract with a buyer, so there's no surprises for either party.

There may be other required retrofits or inspections as well, check with your local government or real estate broker.

Pre-Sale Inspections

It's always the buyer's responsibility to do their own inspections (due diligence) of the property they are buying. But a wise seller will always do their own pre-sale inspections ahead of time.

Having *sold* hundreds of homes in my career, I've come to learn that the #1

reason deals fall apart is because of what a buyer finds during their inspection period. To greatly reduce the chance of this happening to you, I highly advise you get your own inspections done before putting the property on the market. The two basic inspections are a home inspection and termite inspection. A home inspection will generally run around $400-$600 and a termite inspection around $200-$300.

The inspection reports will uncover most minor and major issues. Of course, you probably already know about the major issues but it's good that they will be carefully and professionally documented. Most of these issues will seem so minor you'll probably chafe at the thought of fixing them – but fix them you should. Whether you make repairs or not, fully documenting your home's condition will result in a smoother sale without the need to make concessions to the buyer later.

By providing this documentation up-front, before anyone even makes an offer on your home, the buyer will know what repair issues they may be taking on, before they get into contract. Since they will have agreed to an "as-is" sale, this leaves them little room to negotiate repair work at the end of their inspection period (covered later in Chapter 11).

Some properties require more than a basic home inspection and termite inspection. If your home is on a septic system and you have not had the system pumped and inspected within the past two years, this is something that should be done. If you get water from a well, the well should be tested for both potability and productivity and the tank and pump systems evaluated. There are other inspections that may be warranted, such as mold, asbestos, roof, HVAC systems, plumbing, electrical, and more.

I can't emphasize enough how important these pre-sale inspections are. You will almost always recoup their cost by many orders of magnitude by greatly reducing a buyer's leverage over undisclosed repair issues. It also removes a lot of stress and drama surrounding the buyer's own inspections, because it greatly decreases the likelihood they will discover anything new (and unfavorable) about your home.

Creative Ways to Finance Home Preparation

What if you have more that needs fixing and sprucing up, beyond what a handyman could take care of inside a few days? Earlier I mentioned that it's not uncommon for sellers to spend 1-3% of the sale price on preparing the home for sale. That could be a lot of money, which you may not have on hand. Here are ten different ways you can get the money together to put your home into top-dollar condition:

#1: Have a garage sale. If you're going to be moving in the next few months, you'll probably need to get rid of a lot of stuff. Why not start now? You may have unused vehicles, tools, appliances, jewelry, artwork, collectibles, and other potentially valuable items lying around just collecting dust that don't add much value to your life. Consider selling them at a garage sale, on Craigslist, the Facebook Marketplace, or eBay to add a few hundred or thousand dollars to the repair fund.

#2: Use a PACE Loan. A PACE (Property Assessed Clean Energy) Loan is meant to help homeowners do energy-efficient upgrades to a home (such as solar panels) but in fact can be used for a variety of projects including heating and cooling, plumbing and fixtures, lighting, roofing and walls, windows and doors, and landscaping. These loans are paid on your property tax bill and are easy to qualify for.

#3: Get a Home Equity Line of Credit, Home Equity Loan, or do a cash-out refinance. These loans are harder to obtain than PACE loans, and you need a significant amount of equity in your home to be able to qualify for loans like these. *Most* lenders will want to see you remain with at least 20% equity in your property *after* you take the loan out. However, a few brave lenders have more liberal lending policies and may allow you to remain with just 10% equity in the home after the loan, so shop around. If you *do* end up with just 10% equity in your home after paying for repairs, you might want to ask yourself if you're doing too much.

#4: Do a FHA 203(k) refinance. This loan is different than the loans in item #3 above in that you don't need to be left with 10-20% equity after taking out the cash. An FHA 203K loan give you a new loan up to 96.5% of the as-repaired value, up to the FHA loan limit (which varies from county to county). The catch is that you need to qualify to for the full loan amount, and the interest rate will be charged on the full loan balance. If you drop down below 20% equity, you must pay mortgage insurance too, so this may be an expensive option.

#5: Write checks with a credit card. It's not a great idea to borrow a lot of money with a credit card, but if you pay off the balance in 2-3 months the cost will be minimal, and you can't beat the convenience. Many contractors and handymen do not accept credit cards, but there are companies out there that let you write checks that get paid by your credit card (for a nominal fee). Using

Plastiq (www.plastiq.com), for example, you can pay any contractor, landscaper, or handyman via a check and the charge goes to your credit card – and yes, you should get reward points for it to boot.

#6: Get contractors to extend credit. Some contractors will agree to give short term financing on some of the bill. They'll usually want a big chunk down (think 50%), but some contractors will wait for 2-3 months to be paid the remaining 50% or so of their invoice (which gets paid out of escrow at closing).

#7: Get a contractor to work with a financing company. In the past few years, a number of companies have sprung up to allow contractors to offer financing to homeowners. These companies include Hearth, Acorn Finance and Synchrony, to name a few.

#8: Borrow from your 401(k). With your employer's permission, many 401(k) programs will allow you to borrow from those savings for any reason (including home improvement) up to $50,000 (or half your vested balance, whichever is less). The good news is, you don't have to pay tax on the withdrawal, but you do have to repay the loan (with interest).

#9: Have your broker front the money. A number of brokerages have started to provide sellers with money upfront to cover the cost of repairs, inspections, staging, storage, and whatever else is needed to get a home ready for sale. Notable among these is Compass, with its Compass Concierge program, but a number of other brokerages have similar programs. If your agent's brokerage does not offer this service, have your agent check into third party alternatives, such as Revive (iloverevive.com) and Curbio (curbio.com).

#10: Borrow from friends or family. This is the last item on the list because so many people are reluctant to borrow from people they're close to. However, for some homeowners this will be the easiest, and in some cases the only, source for a short-term loan. Offer to write up and record a formal lien on the property to record the debt, to offer the "lender" some security. You can sweeten the deal by offering them an attractive interest rate or by paying them loan points (say 10 points, or 10% of the loan amount, either up front or upon repayment).

The Disclosure Package

Building a complete disclosure package before listing a home is something not all sellers take the time to do, and this neglect usually ends up costing them a ton of money, time, and stress. I help sellers build a thorough disclosure package and have it available for buyers on Day 1. I do this to eliminate surprises, save time, increase certainty in the buyer's eyes, and reduce friction on the way to a successful and quick closing.

A full disclosure package is extremely important. That's because a homeowner selling their home is required to disclose any *material facts* he or she knows about the condition of the property. But what constitutes a material fact?

As relates to California real estate sales, a material fact is one that a "reasonable person" would believe affects the value or desirability of the property. Obviously then, the term is somewhat subjective. A scratch on the floor in the corner of a room would probably be considered immaterial, but water in the crawlspace underneath a home could quite possibly be considered a material fact by reasonable people.

When you are asking yourself if something is a "material fact" that must be disclosed, a good rule of thumb is: if you're even asking the question, *you should disclose it.*

Fortunately, the California Association of REALTORS (C.A.R.) has a standard set of forms which a seller should fill out. These forms ask a series of questions about the property, with "yes" or "no" answers (though "yes" answers require an explanation). Most of these questions found their way onto these forms because somebody at some point got sued for having failed to disclose the issue covered by the question.

When filling out these disclosure forms, my advice is to be diligent. Much better to disclose too much than not enough. I tell my clients they shouldn't have any fear about disclosing anything, because the decision to buy a home is largely an emotional one, and to be honest, many buyers and agents don't look at these forms too closely.

However, in the event of a lawsuit after the sale closes, the first place the buyer's attorney is going to look is at these forms. If you've failed to disclose some material fact of which the buyer can show you were probably aware of, you could be in for some significant legal issues.

Aside from the standard Realtor® forms, there will be standard disclosure forms that the State of California, local governments, and the seller's real estate brokerage will require that the seller make available to the buyer. Most of them do not require anything more on them than the seller's signature, as they fall under the category of "boilerplate" disclosures and advisories.

In addition to the standard disclosure forms and documentation, the complete disclosure package should include copies of all the inspection reports you have on the property. That includes old ones if you still have them, from when you purchased the property, and new ones you have hopefully had done prior to listing the property for sale. You'll also want to include copies of invoices for any significant work you've had done on the property, a preliminary title report, natural hazard disclosure report (required throughout California), any HOA documentation as required by law, insurance claims history, and a few months of utility bills as well.

A complete disclosure package should also include all government records for the property – the permit history, any history of building code or planning violations, assessor's data, etc. If your home has a well or a septic system, include not just a current report but all the historical records as well, which may be obtained from your city or county's environmental health department.

If your home inspection, termite inspection, or any other reports indicate there is significant damage or deficiencies which should be addressed, the disclosure package should include bids to have the work performed. This is so the buyer will not later be able to ask for a credit for the repair because he didn't know how much it was going to cost.

In summary, a full and complete California Disclosure Package should include all the following:

- Termite Inspection & Home Inspection

- Septic Inspection (if applicable)
- Well Inspection (if applicable)
- Public Records (Assessor, Planning/Zoning, Building, Environmental Health)
- Property Tax Bill
- Natural Hazard Disclosure Report
- Preliminary Title Report
- Parcel Map (showing easements, right-of-ways, etc.)
- Repair Bids (if applicable)
- Invoices for Work Completed (if available)
- HOA Documents (if applicable)
- Most recent 12 months of Utility Bills
- Insurance Declarations / Annual Policy Coverage + Fees
- Insurance Claims History / C.L.U.E. Report
- Local Disclosure Forms and Advisories (e.g., "point of sale" requirements)
- Mold Disclosure
- Earthquake Safety and Environmental Hazard Guide
- Residential Earthquake Hazards Report (2005 Edition)
- California Home Energy Rating Booklet

STANDARD REALTOR® DISCLOSURE FORMS

- Transfer Disclosure Statement (TDS)
- Seller Property Questionnaire (SPQ)
- Lead Based Paint Disclosure (FLD) (for homes built prior to 1978)
- Water Heater/Smoke Detector Statement of Compliance (WHSD)
- Supplemental & Statutory Disclosures (SSD)

- Statewide Buyer and Seller Advisory (SBSA)
- Market Conditions Advisory (MCA)
- Megan's Law Database Disclosure (DBD)
- Agent's Visual Inspection Disclosure (AVID)
- Carbon Monoxide Notice (CMD)

8
Staging

All the work you're putting into your home preparing it for sale is the lion's share of the job called *home staging*. The goal of home staging is to make your property appealing to the highest number of potential buyers by making it appear as attractive – dare I say *sexy* – as possible. Staging is recommended because only about 10% of buyers can see *potential* value; for everyone else, you need to show them.

Most people think of "home staging" as employing the services of a professional home staging company or an interior decorating consultant. In fact, many owners *do* hire a consultant to help with the selection and placement of furnishings, lighting, and décor. If you have a completely vacant home, it may be worthwhile to hire a full-fledged staging company that can rent furniture to you monthly to provide context for the rooms of your house. Studies have shown this is money very well spent, as you'll see below.

Remember, you won't have to stage every room in your home, so the monthly cost need not be exorbitant. Investing a small amount of money in properly staging your home can provide fantastic returns, which show up in a boosted sale price and more cash in your bank at closing.

If you're living in your home while it's on the market, it's usually a question of removing or re-arranging furniture, and a staging consultant can help you make the best decisions about that. But if you'd rather skip the stager, this is something you can try doing yourself – check YouTube for lots of how-to videos on D-I-Y staging.

After you've staged your home, take a walk through it. Are there things that catch your eye, but add nothing to the room? If so, it's advisable to put any such items into storage. If these are things you need while living in the home - kitchen appliances, bathroom hair dryers, etc. - make sure they're kept out of sight, in cabinets or drawers.

Staging by the Numbers

Several studies have been done on the benefits of home staging. For example, a HomeGain.com study in 2012 found that de-cluttering and cleaning alone can yield a 403% return on the cost, home staging yields 196% ROI, lightening and brightening yields 299% ROI, and landscaping yields a 215% ROI.

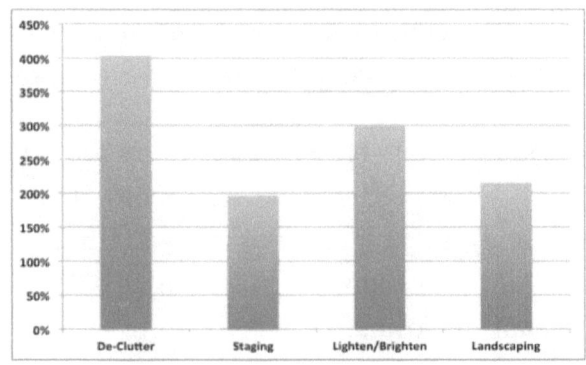

Return on Staging Investment

And per the Real Estate Staging Association, in controlled tests selling identical homes, professionally staged vs. those not staged, the non-staged houses sold in 102 days, while the staged houses *sold* in 45 days.

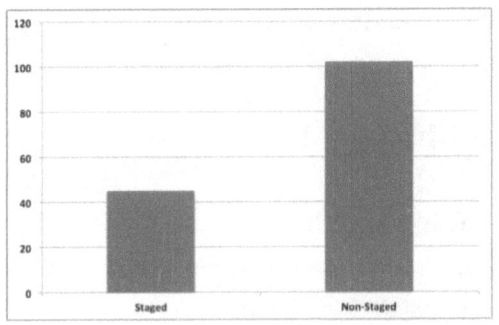

Days on Market, Staged vs. Non-Staged Homes

According to the National Association of Realtors (NAR), the average staging investment is between 1 and 3% of the home's asking price, which generates a higher sale price of 8 to 10%. As you can see, investing just a couple of thousand dollars to make your home look its best will give you a huge return on your investment.

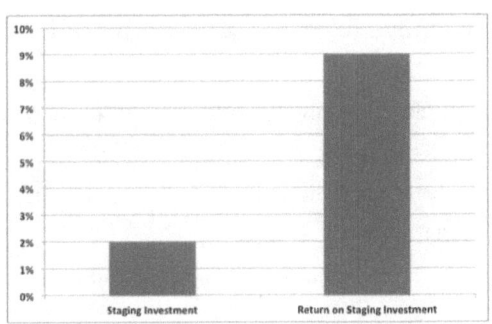

Total Return on Staging Investment

I'm such a big believer in the benefits of staging that **I always provide every seller with a free consultation from a professional home stager**. In cases where the home will be vacant at the time of sale, the stager can also provide the seller with a bid to have the home staged with furniture, artwork, and the like. This will be money very well spent and will be recouped both in a shorter time on market (with lower holding costs) and a higher sale price.

7 Benefits to Staging Your Home

1. Professionally staged homes present and show better than competing houses for sale, including new construction homes and higher-priced houses.
2. Staged properties will sell faster when compared with houses that have not been staged. From the date of listing until the day of closing, home staging shortens this time frame, even in a slow real estate market.
3. Staged properties can increase the number of offers and selling price in hot markets.
4. Buyers view professionally staged listings as "well-maintained".
5. Buyers are more likely to believe that professionally staged listings are "move-in" ready and are more inclined to see staged properties.
6. Photos of professionally staged listings look better on the MLS, as well as in print.
7. Professionally staged listings "STAND-OUT" in prospective buyers' minds.

(Courtesy of the Real Estate Staging Association)

Tip: to learn much more about home staging, including tips for doing it on your own, search Google for "The Consumer's Guide to Real Estate Staging" by RESA, the Real Estate Staging Association.

Love is All You Need

It is imperative that you create a strong *emotional appeal* for your home. That's because homes that buyers *love* sell quickly and for more money. As much as folks try to rationalize or intellectualize home buying –  it's much more about their emotional state, so you need your home to connect with buyers on a gut level. You need to create and reaffirm this connection with the photos and verbiage on the MLS, the view from the curb, and throughout the home itself.

It can be very difficult for homeowners to see how their home's emotional appeal should be improved, because most owners are happy with the way their home looks and feels. It's hard for a seller to see his home through "buyer's eyes" because the seller's brain works to filter out "irrelevant" information – information which the *buyer's* brain may think of as *quite* important.

That's why it's such a good idea to work with a trusted third party – a professional stager, or your Realtor® for example – to help you with this. Do yourself a favor: be open to suggestion and take positive action. You'll thank yourself later.

9
Your Representation

If you haven't already figured it out, I strongly advocate that you be represented by a real estate professional when selling your home. You'll have no shortage of candidates to choose from! Despite what you may think, all real estate agents are *not* the same. You'll need to weigh your choices carefully to ensure you select the right one for the job.

Numerous pollsters have taken America's opinions about real estate professionals. In fact, the well-known Harris Interactive poll revealed that America sees real estate agents and brokers as having the *least prestigious job in America*. It's easy to see why: the real estate profession has a notoriously low barrier to entry. It is *much* easier to get a real estate sales license than, say, an esthetician's license to paint someone's nails.

Careers in real estate have a very high failure rate; it's said that 80% of agents are out of business within the first five years. About half of agents in California sell just four homes *or less* per year! A lot of licensed brokers and agents do real estate on a part time basis, often to supplement a spouse's income. In most areas, 20% of the agents do 80% of the deals. Simply stated, there are a lot of inexperienced, low-skill agents vying for your business.

Pick the Best

What would you do if you discovered you or your child had a brain tumor? As a father, I can't imagine anything more terrifying than some harm coming to my children, and if you have kids, I imagine you feel the same. I know the first thing I'd want is a referral to the doctors at Stanford Medicine – and you probably would too. And if Stanford isn't an option for you, I know you'd fight tooth and nail to get the best care available. You're going to have the same out-of-pocket deductible regardless, so why wouldn't you get the best care possible?

Selling your home may be trivial compared to saving the life of a loved one – but it *is* probably the single largest financial transaction you'll have been a part of thus far in your life. It's surprising to me that many homeowners don't exercise anywhere near the same level of care when selecting a Realtor® to help them get their most prized asset **sold**. *They'll use a friend or family member even when they know they have little or no experience.* Do you want the first-year med student attending you in the emergency room, or the grey-haired seasoned professional who's seen and handled it all?

Questions to Ask Prospective Agents

When you're interviewing agents, there's really only one thing you need to find out. You need to determine, with a high degree of confidence, the answer to one single question: can the agent get you the very best price for your home, on favorable terms, by the time you need the house *sold*?

> **NOTE!**
> Beware an agent who "guarantees" you they can get you a high price for your property! Unless the agent puts in in writing that they'll actually buy it themselves at that price. ☺

Although it's not so important what exactly you ask the agents you interview, it won't hurt to have a few handy questions ready. I suggest asking questions that are a little out-of-the-box and open-ended, so that it gets them off whatever script they may have come prepared with.

To get an agent talking, ask them what they think *you* can do to get the best price for your home - repairs, upgrades, tweaks, etc. See what kind of ideas they can come up with and see if they make sense to you. Importantly, *ask how much that will boost your bottom line.*

Next, ask the agent what *he* can do to make sure you get the highest price. Look for an answer that isn't something they can repeat from rote memory. Don't let them tell you that the market determines the price of the house. If it were as simple as that, there's no need to hire an agent as opposed to just hiring a flat fee discount broker who'll put your home on the MLS for you and let you do the rest.

You want to hear what they'll do beyond putting the home on the MLS, advertising online, mailing postcards, doing open houses, and all the rest. Those are the things an agent should do at a *minimum*. What *else* do they do to get you the best price?

Also, ask an agent how they're different than other agents. What makes them special? Why should you be doing business with them, instead of one of the other agents you'll be interviewing?

Also, consider this: the questions you ask, and even the answers, aren't so important as *the questions the agent asks **you***. Are they taking the time to get to know you, your situation, and how you want your business handled? The questions your agent asks you may be the most important questions of the interview.

Researching Real Estate Agents

Before inviting an agent over to your home for an interview, you should check out the agent to see what reviews they've had on sites like Zillow, Yelp, and "Google my Business." On Zillow, you can see their transaction history which may be incomplete or erroneous, but it's a good place to start.

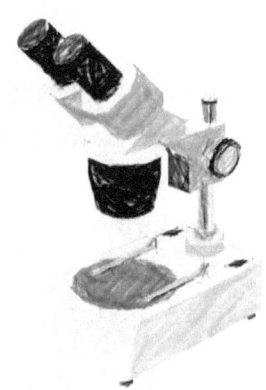

Just go to the agent's Zillow profile. Don't just look at the reviews, also check out the "Listings & Sales" section. This will give you a good feel for how productive the agent is. By clicking on these listings, current or *sold*, you can get an idea for the kind of marketing that your home will receive from the agent.

Even though their transactions may be listed on their Zillow profile, go ahead and ask the agent for a list of the five most recent homes they listed and *sold*, and what the listing and *sold* dates were for those homes. Check to see if the list they give you matches with what's on Zillow and ask about any discrepancies. If there's a home listed as a recent sale on Zillow, but you don't see it on their list, that could be a listing they don't want to talk about – so dig deep on that one!

Pay attention to the photographs you see on Zillow. Do they show the homes in a flattering light? Does the verbiage make you want to get out of your chair and check the place out? You can also ask to see copies of the marketing flyers they prepared for these or other listings and ask to see any virtual tours or videos that they may have prepared. If they don't have any flyers, videos, or virtual tours they can show you, that's a strong indication that these won't be part of the marketing you'll get for *your* home.

Finally, note how many of those sales on Zillow were homes where the agent represented the seller. Helping someone sell their home and helping someone buy a home are different skill sets. If you're selling your home, you want to make sure that whoever you're hiring is someone who has a lot of experience as a *listing agent*. That's what you need if you want to get your home **sold** quickly and for top dollar.

Communicating with your Agent

When homeowners are surveyed after the sale of their property has been completed, there's one facet of an agent's performance that usually gets very high praise - or heaps of scorn. I'm talking about the seller's experiences of communicating with the real estate agent.

Some agents are good at this and keep their clients constantly in the loop. Literally, the client never needs to call the agent, because the agent has kept them apprised of the process, every step of the way. These agents often win high praise from their clients. When you read a lot of Zillow or Yelp reviews, you'll often find that the most glowing reviews remark that the agent had great communication skills.

Selling a home can be very stressful. It's comforting to hear from your agent, knowing he's on the job, taking care of business. You hear what's happening - and if nothing is happening, you need to know about that too, and more importantly, *why nothing is happening*.

When you're interviewing agents, try to get a sense of how good a communicator they are. If you like text messages, ask them if they text. If you like email, ask if they do that. If you prefer that they always call you and you hate text and email, make sure they know that, and that you expect to be contacted at least once or twice a week - or however often you need to hear from them. And if you prefer face-to-face meetings, they should make themselves available for that as well.

Your agent is in the service business. He's going to be well paid for that service. You deserve to get the kind of service you expect for the money you're paying. If you have questions or concerns late at night or early in the morning, a great agent will accommodate you - within reason. Agents are human, after all, and they need rest, sleep, and time off like everyone else. But a great agent will go the extra mile to respond to *urgent* messages day and night, seven days a week.

Being Your Own Agent (Selling FSBO)

A few hearty souls figure they can represent themselves in the sale of their home. Thanks to reality television and YouTube, it doesn't look *that* hard to get a home *sold*! Of course, the magic is in the editing, and it's the parts that get left on the cutting room floor that tell the real story.

The real "FSBO" story shows up in the statistics. Per the National Association of Realtors (NAR) 2020 Profile of Home Buyers and Sellers, only 8% of U.S. homes were sold "by owner" in 2020 (tied for the lowest recorded level since 1981 when they started keeping stats) and *in the Western region, only 5% of homes were sold "by owner."* It should also be noted that 51% of *successful* FSBO sellers already knew their buyer before they sold their home.

Given that over half of FSBO sellers already know their buyers, it perhaps comes as no surprise they're cutting them a deal. In fact, the data from the 2020 report reveal the median sale price of FSBO homes where the buyer knew the seller was $176,700 - versus a median sale price of $295,000 for agent-assisted home sales.

That is a pretty stunning gap! If sellers knew how much money they were leaving on the table by selling "by owner" to a friend, family member, or neighbor, might they think twice? The NAR report also breaks out "by owner" sales where the owner did *not* know the buyer. For these sales, the median price was $255,000, a much smaller gap of "only" $40,000 – or 15.7%

The NAR report shows that the single biggest reason sellers (41% of them!) decide to try selling on their own is to save the commission. It's easy to see why they want to save that money. If most agents in your area are charging 6%, and your home is worth $500,000 – you could keep up to $30,000 in your pocket at closing! Most sellers who are thinking to sell on their own don't realize what the data show, and $30,000 does present a big incentive to find a lower-cost way to sell your home.

In practice, very few FSBO sellers end up saving the *whole* commission. It's very common for a FSBO seller to pay half that (so 3% say) to an agent who brings a buyer for the home. While the seller might not be too happy about it, it makes sense. Again, per that same NAR 2020 report, 88% of buyers purchase their homes with the assistance of a real estate agent or broker, while just 5% purchased *directly* from the seller (the rest mostly purchased directly from new home builders). If you're going the FSBO route, and you're not cooperating with real estate agents, you're turning away the overwhelming majority of home buyers, and that's bad business.

> **NOTE!**
> In 2020, 18% of all sellers received over 100% of full asking price. However, only 6% of "FSBO" Sellers received over 100% of asking price.

In most cases, the FSBO seller won't be saving that 6%, they're looking at more like 3% (the amount they would pay to the listing agent). If you believe that a listing agent provides *absolutely no value* then of course, it makes no sense to pay 3% to a listing agent. But given the number and quality of services a top tier real estate broker provides, the overwhelming majority of sellers in California realize that hiring a professional to represent them in the sale of their home not only makes perfect sense, in most cases it's foolish not to.

If you already have a buyer lined up for your property (usually a friend, neighbor, or family member), selling "by owner" may not be all about the money. That is terrific, and refreshing! But you should realize that it is *mostly* terrific for your *buye*r, not you.

Selling "by owner" to the general public is a classic case of being "penny wise and pound foolish." When you consider that homes which are professionally marketed and negotiated by an agent sell for a margin 2-3 times higher than what you'd likely pay in commissions, the numbers clearly show that "going FSBO" is probably going to cost you.

Discount Brokers

Many discount brokers come and go with shifts in the market, but you've probably seen their signs pop up on lawns now and again. Given their relatively tiny market share, it  seems like most sellers are voting with their wallets and choose to work with full-service brokers and agents. But in case you're tempted, I'd like to spill a little ink and shed some light on how these companies work.

When you start turning over the rocks, you'll find a few discount brokers who trumpet their "low flat fee" commissions. However, this advertising is misleading (surprise!). In fact, the "low flat fee" is for the listing agent and it does not include the commission that you're encouraged to cough up for the buyer's agent. Really, they want you to pay the flat fee, *plus* a very round 3% or so for the buyer's agent.

Not only that, they usually want you to pay the flat fee up front, and that money is non-refundable. If your house fails to sell, you don't get your money back. Traditionally, Realtors are paid for performance – they only get paid when the house sells, so there's usually no cash out of pocket for all your Realtor does for you.

But yes: discount brokers receive relatively little money for listing your home – therefore, *they do not have much incentive to ever get it sold*. Their business model is predicated on double-ending the sale (also representing the buyer, to get the 3% (or whatever) they suggest you offer to the buyer's agent), and to capture buyer leads from your home's listing so they can sell those buyers *someone else's house*. The longer your home sits on the market, the better for them, as they will capture more buyer leads.

It stands to reason that discount brokerages are considered the *bargain basement* of the real estate business. Homes listed by these firms are typically not well prepared, staged, photographed, and marketed. When buyers are out looking at homes and they note a *discount broker* sign in the front yard, most of them subconsciously start thinking about just that: getting a discount.

They are usually aided in this thinking by the presentation of the home itself. A discount broker won't be able to afford to spend the kind of time with you that's needed to position your property to get top dollar. Discount brokers leave sellers on their own to a much greater extent, and it shows. Discount brokers also won't spend the time and money doing first-rate marketing of your home, because there's nothing in it for them. With a discount broker, *you get what you pay for*.

With second-rate preparation, staging, and marketing, buyers just won't have the same perception of *value* for these homes, and so they won't offer as high a *price*. That's the trouble with using a discount broker.

Dual Agency ("Double-Ending" the deal)

Dual Agency in a real estate transaction happens when an agent or broker represents both the buyer and the seller in the sale. In California, this is perfectly legal, and many people wonder just why that is. After all, a lawyer cannot represent both sides in court, so why can a real estate agent represent both parties in the sale of a home?

The answer is simple: in a court room, there's going to be a winner and a loser, it is an adversarial relationship between plaintiff and defendant. A real estate transaction however is completely different: both parties are looking for the same result (the sale of the property from one to the other) and are looking for a win-win outcome.

While perfectly legal, dual agency is not without its problems - so much so that many agents in fact will not represent both parties and will refer one of the parties to another agent. What makes it difficult is that with dual agency, the agent or broker cannot favor one party over the other and must represent both parties equally. They must be fair and honest, and they have a fiduciary responsibility to look out for each client's best interests.

Also, they must not disclose any confidential information from one party to another. For example, the agent may not share how low an offer the seller would accept, nor the highest price that the buyer would pay.

While representing both parties in a real estate transaction can get complicated, it doesn't have to be if the agent is trusted by both sides. The agent must give his best advice to both parties without disclosing any confidential information, and the parties are then free to make their own decisions based on that advice.

Of course, when an agent represents both parties in the transaction, he typically is paid the full commission. In a case like this, some agents may agree to accept a lower commission, to entice the buyer and/or seller to agree not to use another representative. This is legal too, but <u>if a listing agent will agree to do this, it should be written into the listing agreement and noted on the MLS.</u>

The Listing Agreement

To begin formally working with a real estate agent, you'll sign a listing agreement. There are three standard types of real estate listing agreements used in California: exclusive right to sell, an open listing, and an exclusive agency listing.

The **exclusive right to sell** listing is the most common form of listing agreement, and most agents you'll talk to will want you to sign an exclusive right to sell. That means that no matter who brings a buyer - you, your agent, some other agent, whoever - the listing agent gets paid the commission on the sale.

An **open listing agreement** is one that says the seller agrees to pay the agent a commission if the agent brings a buyer, but the owner is free to sell the home on their own, or with the services of another agent. In this type of listing agreement, the homeowner is not actually represented by the agent - the owner is only agreeing to pay the commission to the agent in the event he can find a buyer for the home.

An **exclusive agency listing** is like an open listing except that it allows the agent to represent both the homeowner and possibly the buyer as well, but the seller still reserves the right to sell the property on their own, in which case the homeowner would not have to pay the agent a commission.

Your listing agreement will specify the commission that is paid to both the listing agent, and the buyer's agent. Typically, the commission is split 50/50 between the buyer's agent and the seller's agent, however it is not always the case. The seller can ultimately decide how much commission is to be offered to the buyer's agent.

THE LISTING PERIOD

Many agents will ask you to sign a six-month listing agreement; some will even ask for a year. A lot of homeowners balk at signing a long listing agreement, and understandably so. Their fear is that they will be committed to using an agent who may not get the job done, so they'll want a shorter listing period so they can bail on the agent if need be.

Many agents will tell their clients not to worry about the listing period – they'll let them out of the contract whenever they want. While that may be true, they will sometimes ask the seller to reimburse them for marketing expenses in order to release them from the contract early.

If you're concerned with the length of the listing agreement you've been asked to sign, by all means push back and ask the agent to write a shorter agreement. Alternatively, you can ask the agent to write in the agreement language that gives you, the seller, the unilateral right to cancel the listing agreement with reasonable notice – say 24 or 48 hours.

If your agent won't write up a shorter listing period or give you an explicit and unilateral right to cancel, you can always find another agent. But you should know that a listing agreement can't force you to sell your home to anyone. If you've changed your mind and have decided not to sell, you can ask your agent to pull the listing from the MLS, cease all marketing, and inform the agent in writing that no offers are to be presented to you. Your listing agreement will eventually expire, at which point you will be free to list again with another agent if you so choose.

A Few Words about Commissions

Any discussion about commissions must begin by saying that there is no "standard" commission. Commission rates are not fixed by any organization, governmental or otherwise. In fact, a "standard" commission could be considered price fixing. There is no agreement across the industry between competitors to charge a certain commission.

However, commissions *are* charged for most sales. As a Realtor® and MLS Subscriber, I can easily run queries and reports to see how much commission is offered to a buyer's agent, but not how much the listing agent's commission is.

I did a quick look-up on recent sales of single-family homes in my market, and the average Buyer's agent's commission was 2.49% across 1,120 sales. If the total commission is split 50/50, one can assume that the sellers of these 1,120 homes paid 4.98% on average in commissions. The lowest buyer-side commission percentage in this sample was 1%, and the highest was 5%. However, 1,047 of those listings offered the buyer's agent exactly 2.5%. More on that in a bit.

Please note that this is just a snapshot of time in one market. Next year, everything could change, and commission rates in your market could be higher or lower, today or in the past or future. The most important thing to know, though, is that the amount of commission you pay your agent is *totally* negotiable.

Ironically, one of the main criteria that people use to pick an agent is how *bad* the agent is at negotiating…his own commission. It's understandable that homeowners care about the commission - it's an easy number to calculate, whereas it's much more difficult to calculate all the ways an agent earns that commission. But beware an agent who offers or accepts a low commission. They are essentially saying that their services are worth less than other agents - *and they're probably right*.

The best agents are paid commensurately. If you save 1% on the commission, but that agent brings you in a sales price that's 2-3% *lower* than a top tier agent - how much money have you saved? That's why it's important not to pick your agent primarily on how much commission they charge.

Another thing to understand is that *your* agent only receives a fraction of the total commission. In my market, at this time, it appears the average commission is around 5%. As discussed above, half of that goes to pay the buyer's agent. That is money very well spent – it is imperative that you have someone on the buyer's side who is also incentivized to keep the buyer on track to close smoothly and on time.

That leaves the listing agent with 2.5% - and from that, the agent will need to pay marketing fees, franchise fees, professional photography, video, advertising, printing, signage, taxes and whatever split they have negotiated with the brokerage they work for. The listing agent takes home only a fraction of the commission paid on the sale.

And remember: if your home should fail to sell, your agent gets nothing. They'll often be out thousands of dollars and countless hours, all for naught. That's one reason agents work so hard to get your home *sold*, because failure to close the sale means not just lost income, but time and money spent which is never recouped.

I began this section by stating that there is no standard commission. But then I shared an analysis of recent sales in my market showing that the average commission offered to buyer's agents was 2.49%, and that 93.5% (1,047 of 1,120) of those listings offered exactly 2.5% to the buyer's agent. From that, we can extrapolate that for over 90% of sales, the total commission paid was 5%.

That begs the question: do 90% of agents have the same skill level? Do they provide the same level of quality service? Do they spend the same amount on marketing? Have they sold the same number of homes, or been working the same number of years? Crucially: *do they all get the exact same results for their clients?*

Obviously, the answer to all those questions is no. So, despite significant differences in skill, experience, service level, marketing effort, and numerous other metrics, why do most agents earn the exact same commission rate?

The answer, I think, is that most sellers do a poor job negotiating with their agent on the commission rate. They just accept what's offered (albeit perhaps with a grimace). My recommendation to you is this: ask the agent to reduce their commission by 1%. If they agree, *reject that agent*. That right there is what I'd call a "tell." That's an agent who does not believe in the value they claim to bring for their services.

My advice is, don't pick an agent because they'll take a low commission. It's a red flag, and you should let someone else hire that agent. This is a serious business, and there's a lot at stake. Working with the right agent is money well spent.

10
On the Market

A perennial question for homeowners is: when is the best time to list your home for sale? Conventional wisdom says that spring or summer is the best time to sell. It *is* true that sales volume is high during these months. There are more buyers out at this time - but there's also a *lot* more inventory on the market you'll need to compete with.

From a market standpoint, the best time to sell is ideally when supply and demand are inverted or, in other words, when there are more buyers than sellers. If you have some flexibility with your time frame, you can try to time your market entry to hit it "just right," when competition is light and demand heavy.

As it happens, though, many homeowners do not have the luxury of deciding to wait until the spring or summer to sell, or to monitor the market and put their home on at just the right time, when inventory is scarce, and the buying public is out in force.

The good news is, you can sell your home at *any* time of year with a spectacular result, if your home is properly prepared, presented, priced, and marketed. There are qualified buyers out there looking at homes winter, spring, summer, and fall.

Having said that, there are perhaps a few "blackout" periods where you might want to consider waiting to list. For example, it's not a great idea to list your home for sale the week before Thanksgiving, Christmas, New Year's, or any other holidays or events that mean many potential buyers for your home will be out of town or focused on activities other than buying real estate.

After deciding what date exactly will work best for you to list your home, you're ready to hit the market! All the hard work you've done interviewing agents, completing your disclosure package, preparing and staging the home for sale, figuring out the marketing plan and list price, etc., is about to pay off! The worst of the process is now behind you, and soon you'll reap your reward.

Getting the Word Out

Once your home has finally hit the market, there's a lot more that will need to happen, in the first two weeks especially. While you have hopefully been doing considerable pre-marketing (using the "coming soon" strategy I outlined earlier) prior to formally putting the house on the open market, once the home is listed on the open market, the marketing campaign will hit full stride.

The kickoff for the public selling process is when it is listed in the MLS, or Multiple Listing Service, which brings instant attention to your home. But listing on the MLS is just the beginning. You'll also want to do the full suite of "analog" marketing, as I covered in Chapter 5 on marketing.

Why is it so important to do the old-fashioned marketing, like putting a sign in the front yard, sending postcards and door knocking the neighborhood? It may surprise you to learn that quite often, a buyer hears about a home for sale from a friend or family member who lives nearby – so it's important to make sure that all your neighbors know that your home is for sale.

Your real estate broker should be promoting your home on his or her social media (I know I sure do) – but *you* probably have a lot of connections on social media, too. Be sure you spread the word about your home for sale through your own social media network. It's wise for you to share both the listing of the house itself, and promote open houses on Facebook, Instagram, Twitter, Pinterest, LinkedIn, NextDoor, Snapchat – wherever it is you have connections on-line.

The Perfect Home Sale Schedule

My marketing plan works on a perfect schedule, and it goes like this.

The home will be launched on the market – that is, listed on the MLS – in the middle of the week, on a Wednesday or Thursday. That will give a day or two for the listing to be syndicated out across the web to the various real estate portals and broker web sites, ahead of the first open house which will be scheduled for that weekend. In some cases, we may want to do an open house both days of the weekend.

Following the first open house, the home will be held open one day during the week for the *Broker's Tour*, allowing all the hundreds or thousands of agents in the area to come and view the property at a time when they are already out looking at other homes for their buyers. I also set a public open house for the same time; a lot of buyers come through these "broker's only" open houses too!

At this point, your home will have been on the market for a week or so, and you should have considerable interest in the property. If the price is set correctly, and you've done a good job with preparation, presentation, and marketing, you'll have had a lot of buyers and agents through the door already. It's quite likely you'll already have offers, or "threats" of offers.

It's tempting to accept an offer after just a week on market, and you may choose to do so, depending on your timelines. If you've got some rock star buyers who've made you an offer you absolutely can't refuse – *maybe don't refuse it?*

However, for many homes and many markets, a week isn't going to constitute adequate market exposure. While you may garner an offer or two in a week, you'll probably do better by waiting a bit and working to get another few offers in.

Since I'm a fiend for numbers, I took the time to analyze the sales in my market to see how much the "days on market" affected the sales to list price. Tracking the days on market is very important, because as I wrote earlier, the statistics show that the longer your home is on the market, the less it will ultimately sell for.

When I crunched the numbers, I found that homes in my market which went under contract in *1 week or less* did sell over asking price, at an average of 100.4% of list price. Of all the time periods I studied, the homes which averaged the *highest* sales-to-list price ratio were those that sold between 7 and 14 days on market, with an average sales-to-list-price ratio of 101.5%.

That's why I typically suggest a 10- to 14-day initial marketing period. After the Broker's Tour, the house will be held open again the following weekend, for all those buyers who were not able to see it the first weekend, couldn't make it to the Broker's Open, or who had not yet had a chance for a private showing.

If everything was done 100% in accordance with my marketing plan, there will be an offer – or several – to review the following Tuesday, after the 2nd weekend of open houses. I like to wait until Tuesday so that buyers will have ample time on Monday to get an updated pre-approval from their lender and meet with their agent to write up an offer. Also, it leaves another weekday in case some buyers were out of town for both weekends, or to get a spouse or other decision maker in the home before we review offers.

If there are no offers, don't panic! Sometimes the market hits a lull, and sometimes a home simply requires a bit longer on the market to find the right buyer. If there are no offers available on the first offer review date, the cycle is repeated, with another round of open houses.

The Two-Week Review Cycle

If the home has been carefully prepared and staged per my marketing plan, and if the price of the home has in fact been set correctly, most sellers will have offers to review at the first Two-Week Review Cycle.

The marketing plan is designed to garner multiple offers in this period, because multiple offers always put the seller in a much stronger negotiating position. However, even if only one offer is obtained, the seller is still in a good position to negotiate. The home will not have been long on the market and will clearly be an outstanding value as compared to the other homes for sale the buyer could have made an offer on…but did not.

Remember that "new" is what sells. Even after two weeks, your listing can start to look a little stale. I recommend changing up the main MLS photo, and playing around with the description of the home. Do what you can to catch a buyer's eye who may have passed over the listing the first time around.

If no offers have been obtained after two weeks on the market, another two-week marketing cycle begins, with two more weekends of open houses and another broker's open tour. If after four weekends of open houses, two broker's open tours, and the careful application of my recommended marketing plan no offers have been generated, it is an indication that the price may have been set incorrectly and should be adjusted.

Open Houses

Many real estate brokers despise open houses. They do them for two reasons: to placate a seller who thinks there *should* be open houses, and to meet buyers and nosy neighbors who might one day become sellers themselves.

I have a much sunnier view of open houses. I see them as a great way to get a lot of buyers in your door quickly. Not only does it get lots of buyers through your home quickly, it also cuts down on private showings, which can be highly disruptive for your daily routine and family life.

For a real estate broker, there's little worse than sitting at an open house with no buyers coming through. That's why I make sure that the open houses are well publicized, through the MLS and the web sites which syndicate open house information.

I also promote open houses on Craigslist, Facebook, and Twitter. In addition, I will email my entire database of local brokers and buyers to make sure they've heard about it. I usually incentivize them with offers of treats, like food from a popular deli or bakery. I am not above bribery!

For open house attendees, I also offer a unique incentive to get buyers into your home: for every listing, I have a contest where buyers guess the ultimate sale price of your home. Whoever guesses closest to the final sales price of your home after the sale closes will win a $100 Amazon Gift Card. I find this to be more effective than a guest registry, because I tend to get *real* contact information for follow-up, and valuable feedback as to just how much buyers think your home is worth. Remember, a lot of buyers who walk through your door are quite savvy, and know what homes are selling for. Getting their pricing feedback is gold!

Handling Showings

It's probably inevitable – no matter how many open houses are held – that there will be some private showings. For this reason, your real estate broker will want to install an electronic lockbox for the use of buyer's agents. The electronic lockbox permits timed access to the property – generally between 9 AM and 8 PM.

To get the biggest number of buyers through your door, it's advisable to have liberal showing instructions for agents. That means that agents should be required only to call (or text) you first before they bring their buyer over, and if they don't hear any objection from you within a reasonable time, they just go ahead and bring their clients by.

Some sellers are uncomfortable with that, because they'll want to make sure they have time to tidy up or get the kids or dogs out of the house. That's perfectly understandable, and if that's what you want, make sure you communicate that to your agent, who should be happy to set more restrictive showing instructions requiring whatever period of notice you prefer.

Any time a buyer is in the house, you'll want to control their experience of your home as much as possible. Of critical importance is that you'll want to keep the kitchens and bathrooms clean. You can stash dirty dishes in the dishwasher, that's OK – but don't leave them out on the counters or in the sink. Make sure the bathrooms are clean and as dry as possible, with no damp towels left around and hair dryers and personal care products put away.

If you have kids, that's going to be an extra challenge to get them to keep their rooms clean and their toys put away. One thing that might help is flat-out bribery: give them a bonus in their allowance or some other incentive to keep them motivated to always make their rooms look spic and span.

To maintain curb appeal, consider hiring a landscaper to come once per week for a half hour or so. That's all most homes will need to keep the landscaping looking good, and it shouldn't cost an arm and a leg. Remember, you'll only need the landscaper for a few weeks, just until you get under contract (or perhaps a little longer, just to be safe).

When buyers are in the house, it's imperative for *you* not to be. You want buyers to feel totally comfortable, and at home – *their* home, not your home. I've shown enough homes when the seller is present to know how buyers react. They feel they are intruding and will generally want to leave much sooner than they otherwise would.

If for whatever reason you must remain at home while the buyers are there, be as unobtrusive and as accommodating as possible. Make sure you don't talk business with them. Say *nothing* about the offers and buyer interest you have received, or lack thereof. Limit yourself to talking about the home and leave the rest of it to your real estate agent.

Showing Feedback

Whenever your home is shown, I send an email survey to the showing agent. I encourage the agents to provide feedback on the showing so that the seller knows exactly what buyers are thinking and saying about the home. This feedback is shared with sellers during our weekly discussion of the sale's progress.

I also solicit feedback from buyers at open houses, and if they've registered for my Amazon gift card contest, I'll email them too and ask them for additional feedback if they have any.

You know the old joke about how when you read a fortune cookie, you should always add "in bed" after it? When you're reading your showing feedback, what you should always do is *preface* the feedback with these words: "for the price."

If you receive some "negative" feedback that says for example "The rooms were cramped and the street was noisy," think of it as saying, "For the price, the rooms were cramped, and the street was noisy." After all, if your list price were $1, would you have received any negative feedback at all? Nope! People would be wildly enthusiastic about the great location and cozy bedrooms!

Likewise, when you receive positive feedback, put "for the price" in front of it. So "The kitchen was amazing, beautiful tile work in the bathrooms, and the back yard was great!" you should read it as "For the price, the kitchen was amazing, beautiful tile work in the bathrooms, and the back yard was great!"

If you consistently receive positive feedback, you can rest assured you'll get a good offer, soon – maybe more than one. If all you hear is negative or so-so feedback, you should prepare yourself for a longer time on market and you might want to start thinking about a price reduction.

Tenant Occupied Homes

In my experience, when selling a single-family home, keeping a tenant in place rarely results in the best outcome for the owner. There are a number of reasons for this.

It is difficult, and often "impossible," to properly prepare and stage a tenant-occupied home for sale. Good luck getting a tenant to pack up all their possessions so you can repaint the whole interior! Also, they're not going to want to de-clutter and stash all their personal items away.

I have yet to meet a tenant that is absolutely *thrilled* that the home they are living in is about to be **sold** and they'll have to move. I've never had a tenant ask me if they can have *more* strangers walking through their living space at inconvenient times.

Naturally, most tenants are unhappy that their home is to be **sold**, so it's not surprising that many of them are not 100%

cooperative with the effort. And remember, tenants have rights, and legally require 24-hour notice prior to showings. If buyers are having a difficult time getting in to see the property, you'll have a difficult time getting it *sold*. What's more, I have seen many tenants say unflattering things about the property, and even about the owner. Tenants rarely make good sales agents!

If your home is occupied by a tenant, and your most likely buyer is going to be an owner-occupant, my best advice to you is *remove the tenant before selling the property*. This may mean waiting to list until the lease expires, but if they're on a month-to-month basis, you can just serve them with a 30- or 60-day notice to quit. Of course, you'll want to speak with an attorney about any legal requirements to vacate your property.

But what if you can't evict the tenants, because you really like them, or you can't afford to have the house sit empty? In this case, you need to pull out all the stops and do whatever is reasonably possible to get the tenants to cooperate. For example, I suggest offering them a showing bonus - say $20 off their rent for any day there's a showing, and $50 off the rent to make themselves scarce for the open house.

While I have yet to meet the tenant who's happy the house is to be *sold*, I will give them credit and say that relatively few of them are actively hostile and seek to sabotage the sale. While a few *actively* work against you, plenty will do so *passively*. They do this by insisting on more than their legal rights of 24-hour notice before entering in their premises, and by failing to keep it "show ready" when prospective purchasers come over. A tenant occupied home is never going to look as good or be as easy to show as a vacant or owner- occupied home, and that will impact your sale price.

How much will it impact your sale price? I have never seen an adjustment on an appraiser's report which will show that. In my experience though it's pretty significant. I think that most tenant-occupied homes will see around a 5% reduction in price versus what the same home would sell for, vacant and clean.

Top Tips on Showing the Home

A showing is where the rubber meets the road! You want your buyer to feel very welcome – to feel *at home.* You want them to linger if they can, to form a strong connection to the home. Here's how you can facilitate that:

- Turn off the TV and turn down the radio. Some very soft music playing quietly is OK.
- It's best to have kids and pets out of the house; send them to play in the backyard or better yet in a neighborhood playground.
- Get the adults out of the house, too. Leave the buyers there to their own devices, so they'll be able to speak freely amongst themselves.
- If you're unable to leave when a buyer is seeing the home, make yourself as unobtrusive as possible. Consider waiting on the front or back porch.
- During the daytime, the curtains and blinds should be opened to let in the light; any dark areas should have lights left on for buyers.
- The kitchen sink needs to be empty, and the dish drainer too. No food should be left out.
- Rugs and carpeting should be recently vacuumed, and the floor swept (and mopped too if it needs it!).

- Air out the rooms, especially if you have pets or anyone is a smoker. Spritz some Febreze if need be.
- If you can't leave, let the buyer's agent show your home; let the agent know you are available to answer any questions if needed.
- If the buyers or their agent starts talking business, refer them to your agent. Any talk about price, terms, motivation, etc. should be left to your agent. I've seen owners give away very valuable information to buyers which can be used against them in a negotiation!
- You may get a knock on the door from an un-announced buyer who doesn't have an agent. My advice is *don't let them in*. Who knows who they are? Ask them to make an appointment through their own agent, or if they don't have an agent, ask them to contact your agent to arrange for a showing. They could be completely unqualified to buy your house, or worse – they could be a burglar or otherwise mean you harm.

Selling your Home in a Tough Market

The real estate market is like a pendulum, swinging from cold to hot, sometimes surprisingly quickly and without apparent cause. When the number of homes for sale increases compared to demand, buyers become extra picky. That doesn't mean you  can't sell your home for a fair price. You'll just have to work harder to make it happen.

In a buyer's market, when buyers have a lot to choose from, they're probably not going to buy the first home that meets their criteria and budget. If there are dozens of homes to choose from, don't be surprised if they look at every single one of them. And which of those homes will they choose, if they're in a similar price, location, and of comparable size, age, etc.? <u>They're going to pick the one that looks the best</u>. The cleanest home. The one that feels the most like a new home.

When buyers have a lot of choices, you want to make sure that your home shines and <u>grabs their attention</u>. If you haven't already hired a staging consultant, make sure you get one to come through and give you pointers on what can be done to make your home a standout in a crowded field.

In a buyer's market, you need to make *extra sure* that you have the right price for your home. Did you know that even in a buyer's market, it's possible to have a feeding frenzy with multiple offers and sales over list price? When you price a home right, in any market, you can get a lot of activity and multiple offers. Even back in 2008-2010, when the California housing market was in a total freefall unlike anything anyone had ever seen, it was not uncommon for a seller to receive dozens – yes, dozens! – of offers on a well-priced property.

It will take a bit of a leap of faith on your part, but your best strategy here is to price your home under market value by a few percentage points - say 3 to 5 (as discussed at the end of chapter 6). If your home shines - if it is a standout in the market - buyers will recognize that value and reward you with multiple offers and get your price up to whatever the market will bear. By carefully preparing and staging your home and by pricing it right, you'll be able to get the maximum price for your home, in whatever market.

However, one thing that must be avoided at all costs is to chase the market down. A buyer's market usually means home values are dropping - or if they're not dropping, they soon will be. You do not want to be in a position where you chase the market down through a series of price cuts. That's no way to sell a house - it's painful, agonizing even - and very stressful. This is not a time to be optimistic about the price you'll get. Be *realistic* and set a price at which you know it will sell.

When you do get offers, be prepared to make concessions - even if you have multiple offers. It could be that your best buyer - the most motivated one, who *really* wants to buy your house - needs something from you to make it happen. This could be a closing cost credit, perhaps a bit of seller financing, or you'll need to make a repair for them to get loan approval from their bank. Don't take a hardline approach to any of this. If you can reasonably accommodate a buyer, be open to doing so - as getting the deal closed is in your best interest too.

If you're getting buyer traffic, but no actual offers, consider reaching out to buyers that have visited your home with a reverse offer. Let them know that you will make them a special offer, not to be advertised elsewhere – a discount of a few thousand dollars or a few percent off the asking price. This may be enough to get them to the negotiating table so a deal can be put together.

11
All About Offers

Not long after your home is listed, you should be getting a phone call from your agent letting you know an offer has come in. That's one phone call I love to make!

I need to caution you that not every offer you get will knock your socks off. Most offers require some degree of negotiation to get them where you want them to be. A lot of times, sellers fall into to the mindset that negotiation is a zero-sum game, that when the buyer wins something, the seller loses an equal amount. After all, if the buyer offers $50K less than asking price, that *does* mean the seller would receive $50K less, does it not?

That's true, but I don't view the relationship between buyer and seller as adversarial. Please bear in mind that you and the buyer have a mutual interest – there just might be a few differences to iron out. Consider that the buyer and seller are two parties in the same boat, and they both want to get to the same place. Sure, there will be differences along the way, but with professional assistance on both sides, negotiations don't have to be a grudge match.

Reviewing the Offer

The first thing I counsel sellers to do is to carefully consider each offer. Even if the offer seems like a "bad" one, it's usually worth at least taking a look.

There's an axiom in real estate sales that says your first offer is usually your best offer. I personally don't believe that, but I will say that there's a good chance the first offer you get *could well be* from the buyer who will ultimately offer to pay the most for your home - so give it proper attention. Another thing to remember is that *a buyer's initial offer is very rarely their best offer*. Most buyers are prepared to improve their offer in some way, through negotiation.

Since your buyer's offer is most likely to come from a Realtor®, the offer will most likely be written using the standard California Residential Purchase Agreement (or one of its cousins, such as the Residential Income Purchase Agreement, etc.). This contract is used to sell the sizeable majority of homes in the area, and it is tried and true. It should be noted that it is, however, more *buyer friendly* than *seller friendly*.

Notably, buyers have several ways they can get out of the contract (see below where I discuss Contingency Periods) – but sellers are *not* able to cancel the contract, unless the buyer fails to perform (i.e., do what they say they will do, like fail to release a contingency on time or bring in the balance of their down payment to close the sale). You should keep this in mind when you finally sign on the dotted line agreeing to the sale; you are making a pretty strong commitment to see it through to closing.

Here are the main points of the purchase offer that you will need to pay close attention to:

SALE PRICE

Right near the top of the offer you'll see how much money the buyer is offering, and this will probably be what interests you the most about any offer. While price may be of utmost importance, the *terms* of the deal will often make it or break it, so keep reading.

FINANCING

As I mentioned earlier, about 15-25% of homes these days are bought with cash. If you get an all-cash offer, congratulations! You'll probably have less to worry about in the transaction. Or it could be that the buyer is putting a huge chunk of cash down on the home, which is a sign of a strong buyer.

But there's cash and then there's *cash*. What's the difference? Well, there's cash drawn from a home equity line of credit, cash from a cash-out refinance, cash borrowed from a private third party, etc. These kinds of cash are not the buyer's *cash in the bank*, which means something could go wrong when the buyer tries to access these funds. If your buyer is paying cash or says they have a large down payment, it's important to know where that cash is coming from. Make sure you get and vet the buyer's proof of funds.

You'll probably find that most buyers will have a 20% down payment *or less*. As I mentioned earlier, the average size of a down payment in 2020 among all buyers was just 12%. For most buyers, the bulk of the purchase money will be coming from a traditional real estate loan. For these buyers, you want to make sure that they have a pre-approval letter, not just a pre-qualification, preferably from a local, well-known and well-respected lender.

What's the difference between a pre-approval and a pre-qualification? A pre-approval is where the buyer has already gone through the credit underwriting process. They have been thoroughly vetted and the only thing they need to get the loan is a satisfactory appraisal on the home they want to buy.

A pre-qualification is where the mortgage loan broker reviews the information that the buyer tells them, and determines that *with the information they've been given*, the buyer is *qualified* for a mortgage of whatever amount. However, the lender will *not* have had this information reviewed, vetted, and approved by an underwriter. In essence, a pre-qualification letter amounts to a simple calculation of debt-to-income ratio for a buyer, based on largely unverified information the buyer has provided.

If your buyer is unable to furnish you with such a pre-approval letter, the buyer should be vetted by your agent's lender. If you're working with a top-tier real estate broker, you can be assured that the lender your broker recommends is of the highest caliber. They'll be best able to judge if the buyer can secure the financing they need to get the deal closed.

CLOSING DATE & POSSESSION

Most purchase offers will specify that closing will occur sometime between 30 and 45 days out. Sometimes, closing can be a lot longer than 30-45 days, as when you receive a contingent offer (where the buyer must first sell their current home, before they can close on yours – we'll discuss this in detail later).

Many sellers are fine with a 30-45 day close but will want to remain in possession of the home for some time after that, to give them time to finish packing and moving; this is a matter for negotiation, possibly in a counteroffer to the buyer.

EARNEST MONEY DEPOSIT

The offer will specify the buyer's "earnest money deposit." This is an initial deposit, typically in the range of 1-3% of the purchase price, which is deposited into and held in an escrow account by the title and escrow company, which is considered a neutral third party.

Many sellers assume that the deposit is theirs to keep. Were that the case, there wouldn't be any need to hold it in escrow, it could just be delivered right to the seller's bank. The purpose of the earnest money deposit is just that – to show that the buyer is earnest. To show that they've got some skin in the game.

By keeping a deposit in escrow, a buyer can't just lock up the property and have nothing at risk. They can't just walk away from the contract anytime they want – their earnest money serves to keep them tied to the transaction more strongly than a signed contract. However, per the terms of the contract, the buyer only risks losing their earnest money deposit if the buyer fails to close the sale, after releasing all of their contingencies for the purchase.

CONTINGENCY PERIODS

Virtually all offers will have *contingency periods*. I mentioned earlier that by default, the standard California Realtor® Purchase Agreement gives the buyer a 17 day "inspection period." We also call this a "free look" period, because until that time is up, the buyer can cancel the contract *for any reason* and are entitled to a 100% return of their deposit.

The buyer will also usually have an appraisal contingency (17 days by default) and a loan contingency (21 days by default). The buyer may also have a contingency on the sale of their current home (which I'll discuss further below). Until the buyer releases *all* their contingencies, you should continue to show your home, hold open houses, and attract more potential buyers.

CLOSING COSTS

One drawback to real estate is that it has very high transactional costs – the expense of buying and selling it is not trivial! As a seller, you'll have significant costs – like commission, title fees, escrow charges, transfer taxes and recording fees.

The buyer, too, will have their own closing costs as well: they may also pay title and escrow fees, and have considerable additional costs including loan origination fees, points, appraisal fee, prepaid tax, interest, and insurance – it can add up to quite a lot.

Many buyers seek to "roll in" at least a portion of their closing costs by asking the seller to pay some or all of these costs for them. That's why you need to focus on your "net offer".

Your net offer is the sale price minus any concessions made to the buyer. For example, let's say you are asking $750,000 for your home and you receive an offer of $745,000 – but your buyer is also asking for $10,000 in closing cost assistance (a concession). Your net offer is then $735,000. Your broker will go over all of this carefully with you when preparing your estimated net sheet (I cover net sheets further below).

APPLIANCES AND PERSONAL PROPERTY

The purchase agreement should specify if the buyer wants the stove, refrigerator, and washer/dryer included in the sale. There are checkboxes for these; look for them and see what the buyer is asking for. The checkboxes are easy to miss, and the buyer's agent may have forgotten to check them (just offering them along with the house in the MLS does not automatically convey them to the buyer; the contract is what matters).

Personal property is not *automatically* included in the sale. Personal property is considered items which are not affixed to the property – so an area rug would not be included, but wall-to-wall carpeting *would* automatically be included, since it is affixed to the floor. Likewise, a garbage disposal would be considered an affixed appliance included in the sale. A roll-away dishwasher, though, would be considered personal property not included, but a built-in dishwasher *is* included. In fact, all plumbing and light fixtures are by default included, unless you exclude them with specific language on a counteroffer.

THE AS-IS SALE

As I've written, most "resale" homes in California are sold using the standard California Association of REALTORS Purchase Agreement (the "RPA") contract. This is the purchase offer or contract that the buyer presents to the seller. Even though it is a fill-in-the-blanks type contract, every word of it is legally binding on both parties.

The contract itself is ten pages long, and it contains a lot of "fine print" which most people never even read. One of the most important parts of the contract is the "as-is" language. Your buyer may not even realize it, but when they present an offer on the RPA contract, they're telling you they'll take the property "as-is." The contract states:

> Unless otherwise agreed in writing: (i) the Property is sold (a) "AS-IS" in its PRESENT physical condition as of the date of Acceptance...

The contract also says:

> Buyer has the right to conduct Buyer Investigations of the Property and...based upon information discovered in those investigations: (i) **cancel this Agreement**; or (ii) **request that Seller make Repairs or take other action.**

And to cap it all off:

> Buyer may request that Seller make repairs or take any other action regarding the Property...**Seller has no obligation to agree to or respond to...Buyer's requests.**

What does it all mean? It means that no matter what the buyer discovers about your property during their inspection period, the seller has no obligation whatsoever to make any concessions. The seller doesn't have to do any repairs, issue any credits for repair work, or lower the price to compensate for whatever issues the buyer thinks the property has.

At the same time, the buyer has the right to cancel, if they discover anything – *anything* – that does not meet with their satisfaction. If the buyer cancels within their inspection contingency period, their deposit is refundable per the terms of the contract.

This sets the stage for what can be a tense and fraught negotiation between parties over the buyer's inspections. The seller doesn't have to concede anything around the buyer's inspection findings, but the buyer also can just walk away from the sale if whatever issues are not resolved to their satisfaction.

This is why I'm such a strong advocate for building a complete disclosure package, including pre-sale inspeciton reports paid for by the seller. Doing so will insulate the seller to a very large extent against any attempt by a buyer to get a concession around "undisclosed" issues with the property.

SELLER'S ESTIMATED NET SHEET

Throughout this book I talk both about getting "top dollar" as well as the bottom line. Both figures show up on your estimated net sheet. Of course, the number that really counts is the bottom line, or how much you walk away with from the closing table, after your expenses. I use the same spreadsheet which you will find on the Resources page on my website, so you can play around with your own scenarios any time you like.

RECEIVING MULTIPLE OFFERS

At the beginning of this book, you may recall that I promised you that by using my marketing plan, you could sell your home for more money, and *have fun doing it*. While I hope you will have enjoyed at least *some* of the process thus far, I'll concede it sure has been a lot of work to get to this point! But if we've played our cards right, *the time has come to get the party started!*

I cited a fact earlier than 18% of sellers who listed their home with an agent in 2020 received over 100% of full asking price for their home. How did they do that? In most cases, it's because they received multiple offers for their home. Having multiple offers on a home after a short time on market is the sweet reward for all the work you've put in up until now.

Getting multiple offers on your home is kind of like the holy grail of the sales process, but you need to skillfully work these offers to maximize the sale price. When I am in receipt of multiple offers, I rub my hands, roll up my sleeves and get to work!

I sometimes start by contacting all the agents to let them know that we've received multiple offers, and I'll ask if I've received their client's *highest and best* offer. Just asking this question will often get buyers to improve their offer, without even formally issuing them a counteroffer.

Once I have all the offers collated, I then work with the seller to see what specific counteroffers we want to make to different buyers. We will issue "seller multiple counteroffers" which are great – they are non-binding upon the seller! Even if one buyer accepts the multiple counteroffer, the seller is not bound to it unless they later agree to the buyer's acceptance. Each buyer can be countered on a different price and terms, too.

We must walk a fine line here, because *buyers hate bidding wars*. We want to let the strongest offers know they have a lot of competition while making sure the weaker buyers feel they have a shot. You want to encourage all buyers (even weak ones) to submit an offer, to use as leverage against your strongest buyers. Having to compete against many offers will validate a buyer's decision to pay a lot more than asking price.

Another great thing about getting multiple offers is that you'll have a pool of back-up buyers. If anything should go awry with the offer you accept, you have other buyers ready and waiting to step up. When the winning bidder knows this, they are much less likely to try any funny business around inspection or appraisal issues.

Sifting through a deluge of solid offers is *my* idea of a good time. But what's even *more* fun is watching buyers fall over themselves to offer you a significant premium over asking price. How much over? It's not uncommon to get 10% over asking price *or more* with a well-prepared, beautifully staged, expertly marketed home with the offers skillfully negotiated.

LOWBALL OFFERS

If I never see another low-ball offer in my life, it won't be too soon. *I hate it when that happens!* But sellers hate it even more. Receiving one measly low-ball offer after weeks on market is the *opposite* of the fun you're meant to enjoy with a full and faithful implementation of my method.

It's times like this you need to get your *Ommmmm* on. I suggest you take a deep breath, visualize a positive outcome, and see if there's a deal that can't somehow be put together. It may never be the deal you *want* but may be the deal you *need*.

One word of advice: don't get upset with the buyer for making a low-ball offer. They have at least said they want to buy the place, and that's more than you can say about most of the other people who have come through your house. The way I see it, **a low offer is** *simply an invitation to negotiate.* I have seen many lowball offers turn into great offers, with some skilled negotiation.

CONTINGENT OFFERS

I've already discussed how the buyers will probably have some contingencies built into their offer – the three biggies are the inspection contingency, loan contingency, and appraisal contingency. However, some buyers will also have another contingency: the sale of their current home. This situation is usually referred to as a "contingent sale" which I touched on briefly in Chapter 4.

If you're presented with a contingent offer from a buyer, you have what may be a hard decision in front of you. Here's my advice to help you decide if you should accept a contingent offer or not.

First, you need to determine where that buyer is at in the sale of their current home. These are the questions you need to ask, in this order:

1. Is it even listed with an agent?

2. Is it on the MLS yet?

3. Is it under contract with a buyer?

4. Has that buyer released some or all of *their* contingencies?

Those questions should be asked in that exact sequence. If you get to the end of that sequence of questions and the answers are all "Yes" then you have a relatively "safe" contingent offer to accept.

If the answer to any of those questions is "no" then the "risk" with a contingent offer increases, in the reverse order in which the "no" answer appears. For example, if the answer to question #1 is "no" (it's not even listed with an agent) then then risk is high that this buyer is not going to be able to perform (that is, successfully complete the purchase of your home) in a timeframe that will work for you.

I find that deciding to accept a contingent offer or not is also somewhat dependent on where you are at in the marketing of your home. Has your home been on the market a long time? Are there any other offers on the table? Do you need to close soon, or can you accommodate a potentially longer escrow while waiting for this buyer's current home to sell?

If you have competing offers which are not contingent on the sale of a buyer's home, you might think there's no reason you'd ever want to accept a contingent offer. But there may be reasons after all to accept that contingent offer. For example, is the offer price significantly higher than competing offers? I wrote earlier of the "contingency tax" – and you may anticipate a contingent offer will be paying this "tax." Are there other favorable terms, such as a waived appraisal contingency, or giving you an extended and/or free rent-back if you need it?

There are two main objections to accepting a contingent offer. One is that the deal is more likely to fall apart, since you're relying on some other buyer/lender/agent to close a sale you have very little insight into, and two is that a contingent sale may take longer to close than a non-contingent sale.

Both of those are true, however, there are a couple of upsides to a contingent offer. One I've already mentioned which is that contingent offers tend to be at a higher price than non-contingent offers. The second is that those contingent offer buyers are probably the most-motivated, least-fussy buyers you're going to find.

I've found that contingent offer buyers are the easiest to work with. They have a *lot* riding on the transaction – selling their current home, and buying your home, all at the same time. They will pull out all the stops to make sure that both homes close escrow, because just getting to the point where they have two accepted contracts (the sale of their current home, and the purchase of yours) can be quite a feat.

They are going to do everything possible to make sure the sale of their home closes on time, because they won't want to jeopardize the purchase of your home. Likewise, they probably won't quibble over minor repairs or ask for other unwarranted concessions. Also, more often than not, these buyers are coming in with significant down payments (the equity they've accumulated with their current home) so they may be able to waive their appraisal contingency, too.

In short, my experience has shown me that contingent offers can be a blessing in disguise. Yes, there are risks, but there can be benefits as well. All should be carefully weighed before making a decision on accepting a contingent offer, or letting it go by the wayside.

Negotiation is An Art Form

Negotiation is a learned skill, and I've had a lot of practice. An important tip about negotiating is that it's imperative that the buyer feel good about the deal. A buyer who resents the price and terms of a deal is much more likely to walk away during the sale, and that ultimately could be very damaging to you.

I have found that one of the keys to successful negotiation is that the buyer needs to have a genuine appreciation for the value they're getting *vis a vis* asking price. While the buyer obviously liked your home enough to make an offer on it, they may not understand the full value of the property which is reflected in the price you're offering.

When I write counter offers, I sometimes write a personal letter to the buyer's agent. I'll type this letter into a PDF document on my company's letterhead, so it looks classy and official. I won't write it directly to the buyers, because that would be inappropriate; they have their own representation. But I'm sure that the buyer's agent shows the buyers my letters – because I'm making their job easy, which is to sell the buyers on the house (albeit with price and terms which are usually more favorable to the seller).

These letters I write are amazingly effective at getting buyers to see the how much they stand to gain by coming to agreement on our price and terms. Most buyers and their agents don't have the capacity to cogently defend their own offer price or terms. When they're presented with clear reasoning for a higher price, they'll often come around to accept it if they truly want (and can afford) the home.

While buying a home is an emotional process, the rational side of the brain does play a part as well. These letters help calm the buyer's mind and get them back into the emotional state where they can again feel the love they have for your home. To a large degree, that's what they're paying for – that feeling. And it's priceless.

12
The Home Stretch

You've received one or more offers, negotiated a great deal, and now you're in contract! Congratulations! You're much closer to closing but by no means home free. As they say, it ain't over 'til the fat lady sings (or when the escrow company wires the proceeds from the sale into your bank account). However, because you've  prepared a solid disclosure package up-front and vetted the buyer and their lender, you'll be in the best position possible to achieve a smooth and on-time closing - without any drama or funny business from the buyer.

The Buyer Inspection Process

By default, the California Realtor® purchase agreement gives the buyer a 17-day inspection ("due diligence") period. If you took my advice and produced a complete disclosure package up-front (before any offer is accepted), it is quite reasonable to allow the buyer only a 7-day inspection period. You want to make the inspection period as short as possible, to keep the buyer moving quickly and surely toward closing.

If you have not provided a home inspection for the buyer (or even if you have), your buyer will probably order their own set of inspections once they have the property under contract. This can be unnerving, because no matter how well maintained your home is, you can bet the inspectors will find a whole bunch of stuff that needs fixing (most of which will be penny-ante). However, if you've already had the inspections done, it's unlikely the buyer's home inspector will find anything new of consequence.

It's also good to know that a buyer cannot do any destructive inspections without your explicit permission. They cannot open up walls, they can't pull up carpet or remove stucco. What's more, most inspectors won't so much as move boxes, furniture, or rugs to inspect; they will inspect around those items but may make notes on the report saying "unable to inspect XYZ due to stored items" or some such. By and large, your buyer's inspections will be limited to what they can see with their eyes or test in a way that does not damage the property.

After the inspection reports hit the buyer's hot little hands, they'll go over them with a fine-tooth comb, turning molehills into mountains. A good agent will help their buyer get bids for any repair work called out on the inspection: plumbing, heating, HVAC, roof, windows, the kitchen sink – whatever they can do to help them win a concession from the seller.

Remember that you have not obligated yourself to handle any of the repair work that the buyer's inspectors and contractors call out (it's an "as-is" sale, remember?). But also keep in mind that if the buyer doesn't like what they find during their inspections, they can always *ask* that the seller take some remedy. If the issues are not resolved to the buyer's satisfaction, the buyer may choose to terminate the sale at the time the inspection period is up.

If you do receive an addendum to the purchase agreement requesting specific repairs, remain calm! After doing this hundreds of times, I can tell you that when a buyer honestly wants the house, and the seller genuinely wants to sell, these repair requests can be worked out. As loathsome as it is to get a request for repair, what's even worse is to get a cancelation from the buyer saying they're walking away due to issues with the condition (something that should very rarely happen, if they've had a full and complete disclosure made up-front).

If you are presented with a buyer's request for repair, you have a few options. But before you do anything, remember that per the standard Realtor® purchase agreement, <u>the seller is not even required to respond to a buyer's request for repair.</u> You can treat it as if they never asked and insist that they proceed to remove the inspection contingency and proceed as initially agreed.

Depending on where you are at with backup buyers, you may elect not to reply to a buyer's request for repairs, and instead just issue the buyer a "notice to perform." This is a formal way to tell the buyer "pee or get off the pot!" If the buyer fails to perform (release the inspection contingency and agree to proceed on the price and terms they've already agreed to) within 48 hours, the seller is free to unilaterally cancel the contract and move on to another buyer.

In some cases, the seller may feel that what the buyer is asking for is reasonable, or that it makes good sense for them to offer the buyer *some* concession around repair issues. This may mean that you carry out the repairs prior to closing or provide the buyer with a price reduction or some form of closing cost credit. Just keep in mind that the likelihood you'll have to do this is greatly diminished by doing those pre-sale inspections.

When a seller opts out of doing pre-sale inspections, I always caution them to mentally reserve up to 3% of the sale price to cover these repair issues. Sound like a lot? Too much maybe? *Maybe*, but it's not uncommon to see a $20,000 repair bill on a house that's worth $800,000. Happens all the time – but I don't want to see you getting stuck with the tab!

If you've already had pre-sale inspections completed prior to putting your home on the market, your exposure to issues resulting from a buyer's inspections will be much more limited, and in most cases, non-existent. You can save literally tens of thousands of dollars by making sure your buyer is fully informed about every blemish and wrinkle on your home *before* they go into contract.

Because I make sure our buyer is qualified, vetted, motivated, and my deals are skillfully negotiated, I don't wind up with a lot of broken deals. When a buyer wants to buy, and a seller wants to sell, these issues can usually be worked out and the deal kept intact.

THE TOUCHY-FEELY PART OF INSPECTIONS

I would be remiss if I didn't mention that the buyer's inspection contingency does not extend merely to mechanical and structural aspects of your home. The buyer may walk by at night, to see how loud the neighbors are, and what street parking is like after-hours. They may want to come and "measure for furniture" – more than once (even after their inspection period is over). They may want to taste the water, or even have it analyzed for noxious minerals or toxins (which can typically be filtered out by a filtration system, but whatever).

The buyer may want to "inspect" a lot of things about your house that to you seem trivial, silly, or a waste of time. Also, buyers may pose questions to you about your home that seem irrelevant, or that you feel you've already answered clearly on your disclosure forms.

My advice is to cooperate with buyers during their inspection period (and after) to the greatest extent possible. Even if you have a line of backup offers a mile long, it is usually in your best interest to close with the buyer that you have in hand, versus starting over with another buyer.

Working with buyers is **not** an *us-versus-them* proposition. You and your buyer share a mutual objective; the sale should be considered a joint venture between both parties. So grit your teeth and smile, if that's what it takes. Answer their questions and make your home available for their irksome "inspections." In a few days or weeks, it will all be behind you, forever.

Remember: buying a home is at least as much about how a buyer *feels* about a home as it is about the home itself. You want to make sure that the buyer continues to feel good about their decision to buy your home. *And you never want the buyer to feel like you're hiding something.* Once a buyer loses that good feeling, it's very hard to ever get it back.

If a buyer decides to cancel the contract while their inspection contingency is still open, there's very little the seller can do about it. Under the inspection contingency, the buyer can cancel for any reason, or no reason – they don't have to give a reason, and it's not something that the seller can contest.

My advice is to do everything you can to keep that happy feeling burning brightly in the buyer's heart. Treat them with respect and consideration, like you'd want to be treated if the shoe were on the other foot. You'll be glad you did.

Out of Town Sellers

In today's highly mobile society, it's quite possible you won't be physically near the escrow company at closing. Rest assured, you can close your transaction from anywhere in the United States where a mobile notary can reach you - or any country worldwide with a U.S. Embassy and FedEx!

Seller Sign-Off

Woah, the big day is here! It's finally time for you to sign the closing documents, like the grant deed which will, when it is recorded at the county, transfer the property's title to the buyer. The escrow officer will coordinate a time and date to sign that is most convenient for you. Many sellers will arrange to do this during the workday. Larger escrow companies have multiple offices, and you may be able to go to one of their offices close to your work so you can sign on your lunch hour.

If you can't sign during the workday, some escrow officers will make an accommodation and sign early in the morning or after regular office hours – but don't count on it. Worst case scenario, they'll have to send a mobile notary to your home, office, or hotel room. There's usually an extra fee for this, probably around $150.

You should figure on needing about 30-45 minutes to sign the necessary paperwork. Don't expect that you'll receive the cash from the sale the same day you sign. You'll still need to wait for your buyer to sign their loan documents and get their closing funds in to escrow. Most sellers sign their final paperwork about 5-7 days before the deal closes and they get their money.

> ### What to Bring to the Sign-Off
> - Wiring Instructions – bring a blank check, so that the closing proceeds can be wired to your bank account. You can also opt to receive a check once the transaction closes.
> - Your valid State ID (driver's license or US Passport)

After the Sign-Off

Once you've signed off, the offical closing (when the deed is recorded in the buyer's name at the county recorder's office) should be right around the corner. Your work is mostly done at this point, but the buyer probably has some important tasks ahead: signing loan papers, transferring the rest of their down payment into escrow, and getting the lender to fund the loan. You will be kept apprised of these last crucial steps, but there's really nothing for you to do about any of that.

The only thing you'll have left to do is finish packing! And disposing of any trash, debris, or personal property which you don't plan to take with you. This is something that many sellers overlook until the very end, but you should have a plan for getting all that stuff off the property, because the standard contract calls for it.

The property should be left in "broom swept" condition. There is no requirement to have the property professionally cleaned, although some sellers choose to do so as a courtesy to the buyer.

If you've negotiated a rent-back, you won't actually have to move out on the day of closing. However, if the contract states that the buyer is to gain possession of the home on the day of closing, you'll need to give all copies of the keys and garage door remotes in your possession to your agent, who will then deliver them to the buyer or buyer's agent. If you don't have any keys or remotes, that's fine; you probalby won't been required to provide them.

Make sure that you've stopped utility services as of the closing date, and that you've registered your new address with the US Postal Service. If you have a propane tank, call the company who fills the tank to come out and do a "lock and read" so they credit you for the propane remaining in the tank (that is considered personal property, and does not transfer to the buyer, unless you forget about it). You'll also want to call your insurance company and let them know you're canceling the policy, effective the closing date.

You've now reached the end of the home selling process. You'll probably experience a rush of emotions, and for most sellers, closing the sale is bittersweet. But when one door closes, another opens. You're off to the next chapter of your life, and I wish you the best on the next steps in your journey.

13
The Last Word(s)

Hey, you made it! Thanks for sticking with me 'til the bitter end, and congratulations for being one of the smart ones who educate themselves about the home sale process. It blows me away how so many folks sell their homes with little forethought on how to strategically go about getting the absolute best result possible – but not you! Well done.

As I'm finishing up the second edition of *Get it Sold!* the nation finds itself in the grips of the COVID-19 pandemic. There were many sections of this book I might have further re-written to address the selling a home in this climate.

I refrained from doing so because I believe that so much of selling a home has proven to be about the fundamentals – and in fact, the COVID-19 pandemic has shown that is truer than ever.

Perhaps the biggest change with selling a home in this environment is that open houses are not permitted, and all showings must be by appointment only. No occupant of the home may be present while it is shown.

There's been a big push to virtualize everything and get it all out there on the Internet to the greatest extent possible. I've been doing that and recommending that for years, and the first edition of **Get it Sold!** is little changed from this second edition in that regard.

If there's one thing that selling a home during COVID-19 has taught us, it's that the fundamentals matter now more than ever. Take exceptional care preparing the home, building the disclosure package, and be sure that the photography, video, drones, and virtual tour are standouts. If you follow the advice in this book, you'll enjoy a stellar result selling your home, even during a global pandemic.

I've been fortunate to have helped a lot of people both buy and sell their homes, and one thing I've noticed is that people (especially sellers) are often reluctant to talk to a Realtor®. Even though I'm a Realtor® and I know that many of my colleagues are perfectly wonderful people, I understand the reluctance to *actually talk to one* about selling your home.

I mean, who wants to go see a dentist, right? Really, the last thing most people want to do is visit a dentist. What they *do* want is for the pain in their mouth to go away – and the dentist is the guy you want to see to make that happen.

Of course, a lot of the time, you don't really *need* to see a dentist. Back in the cave man days, did anyone bother with a dentist when they had a toothache? No way! They just did the best they could with the tools at hand – rocks and sticks, but it got the job done. If it worked back then, there's no reason it couldn't work today.

Really, you only *need* to see a dentist if you want to have healthy teeth and gums and live a life without oral pain. That's because what a modern-day dentist will do for you is get you the best result given your dental needs, with much less suffering, anguish, and risk than you'd experience using self-treatment options.

I know, I'm *really* stretching here to equate Realtors® with dentists – dentists make a *lot* more money!

But the analogy is apt: when you need an important job done, and done right – don't try it yourself, and don't hire an amateur. For best results, you should use the services of an experienced, friendly, and honest professional who has a demonstrated track record of success.

It almost goes without saying, but I want to make sure you know that I'm always available for a hassle-free, no obligation and zero pressure consultation. Please don't hesitate to contact me, I'm easy to find any time on the Internet. You can find me quickly and easily at SebFrey.com. Call me, text me, shoot me a message on Facebook or email me – I'll be sure to get back to you right away, especially if you mention that you've read this book and have some questions.

I hope to be in touch with you soon. Until then, best of luck with all your endeavors!

www.ingramcontent.com/pod-product-compliance
Lightning Source LLC
Chambersburg PA
CBHW030749180526
45163CB00003B/953